REVISITING
STEPHEN KING

Critical Companions to Popular Contemporary Writers
Second Series

Julia Alvarez *by Silvio Sirias*

Rudolfo A. Anaya *by Margarite Fernandez Olmos*

Maya Angelou *by Mary Jane Lupton*

Ray Bradbury *by Robin Anne Reid*

Louise Erdrich *by Lorena L. Stookey*

Ernest J. Gaines *by Karen Carmean*

Gabriel García Márquez *by Rubén Pelayo*

John Irving *by Josie P. Campbell*

Garrison Keillor *by Marcia Songer*

Jamaica Kincaid *by Lizabeth Paravisini-Gebert*

Barbara Kingsolver *by Mary Jean DeMarr*

Maxine Hong Kingston *by E.D. Huntley*

Terry McMillan *by Paulette Richards*

Larry McMurtry *by John M. Reilly*

Toni Morrison *by Missy Dehn Kubitschek*

Gloria Naylor *by Charles E. Wilson, Jr.*

Chaim Potok *by Sanford Sternlicht*

Amy Tan *by E.D. Huntley*

Anne Tyler *by Paul Bail*

Leon Uris *by Kathleen Shine Cain*

Kurt Vonnegut *by Thomas F. Marvin*

Tom Wolfe *by Brian Abel Ragen*

REVISITING STEPHEN KING

A Critical Companion

Sharon A. Russell

CRITICAL COMPANIONS TO POPULAR CONTEMPORARY WRITERS
Kathleen Gregory Klein, Series Editor

Greenwood Press
Westport, Connecticut • London

Library of Congress Cataloging-in-Publication Data

Russell, Sharon A., 1941–
   Revisiting Stephen King : a critical companion / Sharon A. Russell.
     p. cm.—(Critical companions to popular contemporary writers, ISSN 1082–4979)
   Includes bibliographical references (p.   ) and index.
   ISBN 0–313–31788–7 (alk. paper)
   1. King, Stephen, 1947—Criticism and interpretation. 2. Horror tales,
American—History and criticism. I. Title. II. Series.
   PS3561.I483Z864 2002
   813'.54—dc21   2001058641

British Library Cataloguing in Publication Data is available.

Library of Congress Catalog Card Number: 2001058641
ISBN: 0–313–31788–7
ISSN: 1082–4979

First published in 2002

Greenwood Press, 88 Post Road West, Westport, CT 06881
An imprint of Greenwood Publishing Group, Inc.
www.greenwood.com

Printed in the United States of America

The paper used in this book complies with the
Permanent Paper Standard issued by the National
Information Standards Organization (Z39.48–1984).

10 9 8 7 6 5 4 3 2 1

Once again for my sister Judith, who shares my love of horror. She has fought many monsters in her life.

Contents

Series Foreword

The authors who appear in the series Critical Companions to Popular Contemporary Writers are all best-selling writers. They do not simply have one successful novel, but a string of them. Fans, critics, and specialist readers eagerly anticipate their next book. For some, high cash advances and breakthrough sales figures are automatic; movie deals often follow. Some writers become household names, recognized by almost everyone.

But, their novels are read one by one. Each reader chooses to start and, more importantly, to finish a book because of what she or he finds there. The real test of a novel is in the satisfaction its readers experience. This series acknowledges the extraordinary involvement of readers and writers in creating a best-seller.

The authors included in this series were chosen by an Advisory Board composed of high school English teachers and high school and public librarians. They ranked a list of best-selling writers according to their popularity among different groups of readers. For the first series, writers in the top-ranked group who had received no book-length, academic, literary analysis (or none in at least the past ten years) were chosen. Because of this selection method, Critical Companions to Popular Contemporary Writers meets a need that is being addressed nowhere else. The success of these volumes as reported by reviewers, librarians, and teachers led to an expansion of the series mandate to include some writers with wide critical attention—Toni Morrison, John Irving, and Maya Angelou, for example—to extend the usefulness of the series.

The volumes in the series are written by scholars with particular expertise in analyzing popular fiction. These specialists add an academic focus to the popular success that these writers already enjoy.

The series is designed to appeal to a wide range of readers. The general reading public will find explanations for the appeal of these well-known writers. Fans will find biographical and fictional questions answered. Students will find literary analyses, discussions of fictional genres, carefully organized introductions to new ways of reading the novels, and bibliographies for additional research. Whether browsing through the book for pleasure or using it for an assignment, readers will find that the most recent novels of the authors are included.

Each volume begins with a biographical chapter drawing on published information, autobiographies or memoirs, prior interviews, and, in some cases, interviews given especially for this series. A chapter on literary history and genres describes how the author's work fits into a larger literary context. The following chapters analyze the writer's most important, most popular, and most recent novels in detail. Each chapter focuses on one or more novels. This approach, suggested by the advisory board as the most useful to student research, allows for an in-depth analysis of the writer's fiction. Close and careful readings with numerous examples show readers exactly how the novels work. These chapters are organized around three central elements: plot development (how the story line moves forward), character development (what the reader knows of the important figures), and theme (the significant ideas of the novel). Chapters may also include sections on generic conventions (how the novel is similar to or different from others in its same category of science fiction, fantasy, thriller, etc.), narrative point of view (who tells the story and how), symbols and literary language, and historical or social context. Each chapter ends with an "alternative reading" of the novel. The volume concludes with a primary and secondary bibliography, including reviews.

The alternative readings are a unique feature of this series. By demonstrating a particular way of reading each novel, they provide a clear example of how a specific perspective can reveal important aspects of the book. In the alternative reading sections, one contemporary literary theory—way of reading, such as feminist criticism, Marxism, new historicism, deconstruction, or Jungian psychological critique—is defined in brief, easily comprehensible language. That definition is then applied to the novel to highlight specific features that might go unnoticed or be understood differently in a more general reading. Each volume defines two or three specific theories, making them part of the reader's understanding of how diverse meanings may be constructed from a single novel.

Taken collectively, the volumes in the Critical Companions to Popular Contemporary Writers series provide a wide-ranging investigation of the complexities of current best-selling fiction. By treating these novels seriously as both literary works and publishing successes, the series demonstrates the potential of popular literature in contemporary culture.

Kathleen Gregory Klein
Southern Connecticut State University

Acknowledgments

I would like to thank my students who have shared their love of Stephen King with me. I would also like to thank my friends and colleagues for their kind comments about the first edition.

REVISITING
STEPHEN KING

The Life of Stephen King

Stephen King's life and work are examples of both traditional and modern views of the "American Dream." His early life is similar to the stories we heard when we were young about children who are born in poverty and grow up to be president or head of a big company. Such elements of his early life as his moving from city to city and his being raised by a single parent are also hardships familiar to many contemporary Americans. In order to understand King's achievements and his outlook towards his work, we have to examine both sides of the "American Dream" as it works itself out in his life.

While many people envy his fame and even the money he has made from his writing, few are willing to appreciate how hard he worked to achieve them. King was not an "overnight success." He suffered through many years of rejections before achieving his current popularity. And even success did not bring him a life of ease. As he has recently revealed, he struggled with addiction. King also had to fight his way back from an accident that could have ended his life. He survived and has become one of America's most popular contemporary authors, one of the few who are easily recognized by the general public. Even before he appeared in cinematic adaptations of his work, fans knew him.

At the same time, King manages to live a relatively normal life because he chooses to remain in Maine. While he tries to guard his privacy so that he has the time to continue writing, he has been very generous with interviews. He has also given us reflections on his life and work in ar-

ticles, in introductions to his books, and in his non-fiction study of the
horror genre, *Danse Macabre*. How he deals with fame and his work in
the horror genre is revealed in an essay called "On Becoming a Brand
Name," his foreword to an early collection of essays about his oeuvre,
Fear Itself: The Early Works of Stephen King. He shares his views on writing,
his problems with addiction, and the accident in his book *On Writing: A
Memoir of the Craft*.

EARLY LIFE

King is a member of the baby-boom generation. After Donald Edwin
King returned from World War II, he and his wife, Nellie Ruth Pillsbury
King, adopted a son, David Victor, on September 14, 1945. Doctors had
told them they could not have children of their own. But as many adop-
tive parents have discovered, the doctors were wrong. Stephen was born
two years later, on September 21, 1947, at the Maine General Hospital
in Portland (Beahm, *Stephen King Story* 15). King's mother was of Scottish
descent and claimed to be related to the famous Pillsburys who make
flour and related items. "The difference between the two branches, Mom
said, was that the flour-Pillsburys moved west to make their fortune,
while our people stayed shirttail but honest on the coast of Maine"
(*Danse* 98). While not famous, his grandmother was the first woman to
graduate from Gorham Normal School, and his grandfather worked for
a short time for the artist Winslow Homer (*Danse* 98). King's father's
family came from Ireland and settled in Peru, Indiana.

When Stephen was two years old, his father went out for a pack of
cigarettes and never returned. While King never knew his father, he saw
photographs of him and is certain he inherited his poor eyesight (*Danse*
99). After his father left, his mother supported the family with a variety
of jobs. They had few material possessions but never went hungry. "She
was a talented pianist and a woman with a great and sometimes eccentric
sense of humor and somehow she kept things together, as women before
her have done and as other women are doing even now as we speak"
(*Danse* 99). The family moved around the country for the next nine years,
always remaining poor. They stayed with relatives, most often those on
his mother's side, in such cities as Malden, Massachusetts; Stratford,
Connecticut; Chicago, Illinois; West De Pere, Wisconsin; and Fort Wayne,
Indiana (Beahm, *Stephen King Companion* 16). The family finally returned
to Durham, Maine, when his grandparents were in their eighties, and
his mother was hired to take care of them (*Danse* 17).

King describes his first real encounter with horror at the age of four. He wanted to listen to a radio adaptation of Ray Bradbury's story "Mars Is Heaven" on the series *Dimension X*. His mother didn't want him to hear the story because he was too young, but he listened through the door. That night he was too frightened to sleep in his bed and slept where he could see the light from the bathroom (*Danse* 120–21).

King also notes some of the literary influences from this period in his life. He always read a great deal. When the family returned to Durham, King was able to explore a relative's attic, where he found a collection of his father's things including a reel of movie film and boxes of books, one of which contained an H.P. Lovecraft anthology of horror stories. "So that book, courtesy of my departed father, was my first taste of a world that went deeper than the B-pictures which played at the movies on Saturday afternoon" (*Danse* 101–2). Even though the books disappeared in a couple of weeks (King suspected a disapproving aunt), Lovecraft provided an introduction to the world of horror literature.

King credits the *Ripley's Believe It or Not!* series of paperbacks published by Pocket Books with introducing him to the world of amazing facts. "It was in *Ripley's Believe It or Not!* that I first began to see how fine the line between the fabulous and the humdrum could sometimes be, and to understand that the juxtaposition of the two did as much to illuminate the ordinary aspects of life as it did to illuminate its occasional weird outbreaks" (*Nightmares* 3).

Films, too, were an important influence for the young King. He remembers seeing his first movie, *Creature from the Black Lagoon*, at a drive-in when he was about seven. King knew the creature was not real, but he also knew that a more realistic version would visit him at some point in his dreams (*Danse* 104). King sees this example of how children juggle their belief in the world of the imagination as the key to their openness. Adults have lost their ability to expose themselves to these possibilities. A successful horror film returns us to that childhood state where we can believe in the possibility that the monster exists (*Danse* 105–6). Even when King watches the same film twenty-two years later with his son, he still has enough imagination for the film to have an effect on him (*Danse* 110).

While King believes that writers are made through hard work, he describes other incidents from his childhood that had an effect on the direction of his work. He tells of dowsing with his Uncle Clayton. Once Uncle Clayton found the water, he let King hold the dowsing stick, and King felt it move at the same spot. He compares talent to the water, which is there but must be developed (*Danse* 94–97).

King wrote his first horror story when he was seven. Later he got an old Underwood typewriter whose letters kept breaking. Like Paul Sheldon in *Misery*, he had to fill in some of the letters by hand. King began submitting stories to magazines when he was twelve (Winter, *Art* 18–19). He was also interested in real crime. He was fascinated with Carl Starkweather, who went on a murder spree across the country, and kept a scrapbook of clippings about him. He both loved and was terrified of this real killer (Winter, *Art* 20).

The town of Durham was also important in King's early life. It is the basis for Derry, Castle Rock, 'salem's Lot, and all the other small Maine towns in his work. The Harmony Grove Cemetery becomes Harmony Hill in *'Salem's Lot*. A dead body he saw being pulled out of a lake reappears in the short story "The Body" in *Different Seasons*. King attended a one-room schoolhouse in Durham, another element of the image of the "American Dream" in his life. He graduated at the top of his class of three in the spring of 1962 (Beahm, *Stephen King Story* 29). King had a rather average high school experience. In his youth he was heavy and not very athletic, like his hero in *It*, Bill Denbrough. The town hired an old limousine to take the students to Lisbon High School in Lisbon Falls. One of the two young women who shared the limo became a model for Carrie. King generally got good grades, except in chemistry and physics, and played left tackle in football and rhythm guitar in a rock band. He was best known for his writing talent (Beahm, *Stephen King Story* 29). He published his first story, "I Was a Teenage Grave Robber," in a comics fan magazine, *Comics Review*, in 1965 (Winter, *Art* 22). He wrote his first full-length work, *The Aftermath*, during this period, but he was best known for a high school newspaper called *Village Vomit*, which once earned him a three-day suspension from school (Winter, *Art* 22).

COLLEGE YEARS

During the summer of 1966, after graduating from high school, King started writing *Getting It On*, which he later published under the pseudonym Richard Bachman as *Rage*. This novel about an outsider who holds his high school class hostage is the first evidence of King's mature writing. He uses his own feeling of not fitting in to create an original expression of the high school experience. After high school shootings at such places as Columbine High School in Colorado made the novel seem prophetic, he has withdrawn it from publication.

Even though he was accepted at Drew University, a Methodist college near New York City, King could not afford to go there and went instead to the University of Maine in Orono. During his freshman year he sold his first story to a real magazine. *Startling Mystery Stories* published "The Glass Floor" (Winter, *Art* 23). While a freshman he also completed *The Long Walk*, which he later published as Richard Bachman. His professors were impressed with this novel. King submitted it to a competition and was crushed when it did not win (Beahm, *Stephen King Story* 40). The only other novel he completed during college was *Sword in the Darkness*, which has not been published.

King gained the most from his literature classes during his college years. He was strongly influenced by such naturalist writers as Thomas Hardy, Jack London, and Theodore Dreiser (Winter, *Art* 23). He also read a lot of popular fiction outside of the classroom. While he felt that his creative writing classes actually inhibited him, he greatly appreciated the support of his professors, who were very positive about his literary efforts. One helped him get an agent, and even though *Sword in the Darkness* never sold, King did publish several stories in *Ubris*, a college literary magazine.

College also brought King in contact with new ideas. He entered the university a conservative, but the activism of colleges in the 1960s affected him. The student reaction to events in Vietnam changed his view of the world, and he joined in student protests. He revisits his experiences as a student during the Vietnam War in "Hearts in Atlantis," in the book of the same name. In its opening, the narrator of this story presents the changes he has experienced. He arrived at the university with a Goldwater sticker on his car. He leaves with no car. "What I did have was a beard, hair down to my shoulders, and a backpack with a sticker on it reading RICHARD NIXON IS A WAR CRIMINAL" (257). The narrator realizes that the late sixties were a tremendous force in changing the lives of the students who experienced them. King also saw horror fiction as an appropriate response to the times. He recognized that a film like *The Exorcist* was a parable for parents of how their children were being transformed into monsters (Beahm, *Stephen King Story* 46). He expressed his views on a variety of subjects in a column he wrote for the school newspaper, "King's Garbage Truck" (Winter, *Art* 25).

King had to work to support himself while at the university. In his senior year he had a job at the library, where he met his future wife, Tabitha Jane Spruce. While it was not love at first sight, they did date. Tabitha says she was more impressed with him than he was with her. She also describes King's extreme poverty at this time. "Talk about going to college poor . . . this guy was going to college the way people did in the twenties and thirties. He had nothing to eat, he had no money, he had no clothes; it was just incredible that anybody was going to school under those circumstances, and even more incredible that he didn't care" (Winter, *Art* 26). King began work on the first story in The Dark Tower series with one of the reams of colored paper that were kept in the library. But the story had to wait while King tried to find a job. He graduated on June 5, 1970, with a B.S. in English, a minor in speech, and a secondary-school teaching certificate (Beahm, *Stephen King Story* 50). At the time there were not a lot of jobs for English teachers. King pumped gas and then worked in a laundry, which provided the background for his story "The Mangler." He also began writing stories for various men's magazines. *Cavalier*, in particular, published many of his horror stories.

STRUGGLE AND FIRST SUCCESS

King struggled professionally, but his private life was going well. He married Tabitha on January 2, 1971, in Orono. Tabitha was Catholic, so the wedding was held at a Catholic church, but the reception was held at a Methodist church to give King's religion equal time (Beahm, *Stephen King Story* 54). Tabitha graduated from the University of Maine in May 1971. She could not find a job in her field either and worked as a waitress at a Dunkin' Donuts in Bangor, Maine (Beahm, *Stephen King Story* 55). King constantly acknowledges Tabitha's importance to him both personally and in his career. She is his partner in the deepest sense of the word.

When King decided to try publishing *Getting It On*, his novel about high school, he sent it to Doubleday because they published so many books. He had also recently read *The Parallax View* by Loren Singer, and he thought the editor of that book might be interested in his kind of writing. Singer's editor was sick when King's book arrived, so it was given to Bill Thompson, who liked the novel but couldn't persuade Doubleday to publish it. King was disappointed by this rejection and took a teaching job for $6,400 a year at Hampden Academy, where he had done his student teaching.

By this point the Kings had two children and were living in a trailer in Hermon, Maine. There was so little space that King wrote at a child's desk in the laundry room. "Tabby juggled the bills with the competent but scary expertise of a circus clown juggling tennis racquets; the transmission on our senile 1965 Buick Special began to whine, then to groan, then to chug and hitch; and as winter came in, the snow-mobiles began to buzz across the fields" (Underwood and Miller, *Fear Itself* 19–20). King was desperate and didn't have any ideas. He had not thought of writing a horror novel, even though he had been selling horror stories. He decided to work on a short story he had begun the summer before called "Carrie" (Underwood and Miller, *Fear Itself* 20). King thought the opening scene in the women's shower unrealistic, so he threw the pages in the wastebasket. Luckily Tabitha retrieved them and urged him to continue. King persisted even when it looked as if the work would be novella length—longer than a short story but shorter than a novel—which would make it unsellable (Underwood and Miller, *Fear Itself* 21–22).

In January 1973 King sent *Carrie* to Thompson at Doubleday. Thompson suggested some revisions, which King realized would strengthen the book. Thompson liked the rewrite, and in February King went to New York. A typical country hick, he bought a map and got blisters on his feet walking to the restaurant for lunch because he had new shoes. His neck was stiff from looking up at the buildings. He had not slept on the bus and got drunk on two gin and tonics. "I had never been so determined to make no glaring social *gaffe* and never so convinced (at least since the night of my high school junior prom) that I would make one. To top off everything, I ordered fettuccini, a dish bearded young men should avoid" (Underwood and Miller, *Fear Itself* 25). Somehow King did not destroy his chances with this performance. A month later Tabitha used a neighbor's phone to call him at school with the news that Doubleday was going to publish *Carrie*. The publisher offered him an advance of $2,500, which was a good amount for a first novel. The Kings used the money to buy a new car. But the real money for *Carrie* came with the paperback sales.

King knew that the hardcover sales would not be good for a new author, especially for a horror story. Publishers tend to promote what they consider serious fiction in hardcover, especially when dealing with a first novel. Paperback publishers are more interested in popular fiction. *Carrie* attracted the attention of New American Library, which bid $400,000 for the paperback rights. According to its standard contract, Doubleday kept half the money from the paperback sale of a novel. (This policy would later lead King to leave the publisher.) King couldn't believe the amount of the sale and had to call Thompson back. For the next few weeks, he was certain someone had made a mistake (Underwood and Miller, *Fear Itself* 28), and during this period he worked on a suspense novel that he didn't sell. He got the idea for his second novel during a dinner conversation with Tabitha and his friend Chris Chesley. King was teaching *Dracula*, and they discussed what would happen if the Count appeared in the twentieth century. While King was sure the FBI would find him right away, Chris and Tabitha suggested that he look more closely at some of the small towns around them (Underwood and Miller, *Fear Itself* 29). A vampire's actions could easily be concealed in these communities, which have little contact with the outside world. King feels that teaching Thornton Wilder's play *Our Town* gave him additional insight into small-town life that was helpful in creating the setting of *'Salem's Lot*. King finished this novel, originally called *Second Coming*, just before he learned about the paperback sale of *Carrie*. Thompson was concerned that King would be typecast as a horror writer, but King was not worried, knowing it was the kind of book he could write best.

In 1973, before *Carrie* was published, King's mother died from cancer after a long illness. King presents one view of her death in "The Woman in the Room," published in *Night Shift*, his first collection of short stories, which he dedicated to her. His mother had encouraged King's writing and often struggled to give him the postage to mail out his short stories. She knew about the sale of *Carrie*, and he was able to give her a pre-publication copy of the book, but she never lived to see the success he has achieved. His greatest tribute to Ruth Pillsbury King is *Dolores Claiborne* (1993). This novel, also dedicated to her, is a beautiful examination of the life of a hardworking mother in Maine. He also describes her death in *On Writing* in the context of his struggle with alcohol (93). He confesses that he gave a decent eulogy even though he was drunk (94).

In his article "On Becoming a Brand Name," King explains that publishers like to be able to bounce back and forth between hardcover editions of one book and paperback versions of another because each creates new interest in the author (Underwood and Miller, *Fear Itself* 31–32). With the sale of *Carrie*, King decided to leave teaching to become a full-time writer. Although he didn't want to leave his students and was considered a good teacher, King had always wanted to be a writer. By the time *'Salem's Lot* was published in 1975, he was on his way to the major success he has achieved as an author.

After writing two books with Maine settings, King decided to live somewhere else for a while. The family moved to Boulder, Colorado, in the summer of 1974 and lived there for a year before returning to Maine (Beahm, *Stephen King Companion* 67). King tried to write a novel about the Patty Hearst kidnapping, but he could not develop the story. He and Tabitha decided to go away for a weekend and took the suggestion of friends to try the Stanley Hotel. They arrived the day before the hotel closed for the winter. They were the only guests, and King was inspired by what he saw at the hotel. He immediately began work on a book called *The Shine*. (The name was changed to *The Shining* when King learned that "shine" was a disparaging term applied to African Americans.) *The Shining* was the first King novel to become a hardcover best-seller (Underwood and Miller, *Fear Itself* 41). With its publication King was becoming a brand name, an author whose name alone would sell the book.

THE SUCCESSFUL AUTHOR

King's rise to fame and fortune after hard work and rejection reaffirms our belief in the "American Dream." While King's novels often explore the dark side of American life, he personally continues to embody much of what is considered best in this country. Unlike some people who grow up poor and suddenly become wealthy, King does not seem to have been spoiled by success. He continues to work as hard as he did before his early achievements. He still approaches his writing with discipline. King likes to write to loud rock and roll music, which blocks out other sounds and helps him concentrate. When he is involved with a project, he writes every morning for at least three hours and tries to complete ten pages every day (*On Writing* 153–54). He spends the rest of his workday dealing with such other aspects of his career as giving interviews and answering fan mail.

King lets his first draft sit for a while. On the second, he pays attention to the details, fixing things like character motivation while also looking for the major themes (*On Writing* 213–14). Only after he has completed this revision does he show the work to a few select people. His first and most important reader is his wife (*On Writing* 215). King wants his work to be accessible and says, "It should be like a good car. You have a good car and when the engine is in tune and running right, you can't hear the motor, but that doesn't mean it isn't doing its work" (Underwood and Miller, *Bare Bones* 75).

King has been such a prolific writer that at certain points in his career his publisher wanted to limit the number of books that came out each year and avoid having King typecast with the horror genre. In order not to overuse his name, King devised the alter ego, Richard Bachman. From 1977 to 1997 he wrote six books under this name: *Rage, The Long Walk, Roadwork, The Running Man, Thinner,* and *The Regulators*. In these novels he seems to create both simpler and more violent worlds than those found in the rest of his fiction.

King is realistic about his everyday life. He remains in Maine and is actively involved with his wife and three children, Naomi, Joe, and Owen. "You know, I've got three kids and I've changed all their diapers in the middle of the night, and when it's two o'clock in the morning and you're changing something that's sort of special delivery with one eye shut you don't *feel* famous" (Underwood and Miller, *Bare Bones* 1). He also feels that staying in Maine has helped him keep a perspective on his life. "And I live in Bangor, Maine which is not a town calculated to make anybody feel famous. The only claim to fame is a big plastic statue of Paul Bunyan. You just live there and keep your head down" (Underwood and Miller, *Bare Bones* 1–2). King is an avid baseball fan, and his team is the Boston Red Sox. He marks the year by the opening and closing of the baseball season, shaving his beard when the season opens and growing it again for the winter after the World Series.

During the 1980s King continued to publish regularly, and his fame increased. People also began to write books about him. His books were making so much money that he took a cash advance of only $1 for *Christine*. He felt that would free up advance money for less well-known authors; it also meant he would receive royalties sooner (Beahm, *Stephen King Story* 108). His increased fame also led to discovery of his pseudonym. When *Thinner* was published people began to notice stylistic similarities between King and Bachman, since *Thinner* was a recent creation and had more of King's mature style (Beahm, *Stephen King Story* 122–23).

Fame has advantages and disadvantages for King. His appearance on the October 6, 1985, cover of *Time* magazine confirmed his place in American popular culture (Beahm, *Stephen King Story* 133). King also tells about having dinner at a restaurant with one of his idols, Bruce Springsteen. A young woman dining with her family at a nearby table approached King and Springsteen. Springsteen took out a pen to sign an autograph. But she was interested in King and told him she had read every one of his books (Beahm, *Stephen King Story* 133). Not all of his encounters with fans have been as positive. The Kings had to fence in their Bangor home and then take even stronger security measures when a fan actually broke into the house and claimed to have a bomb. Tabitha was able to get out of the house, and the bomb was not real (Beahm, *Stephen King Story* 161).

Recently King admitted to other problems often associated with fame and with the writer's life—alcohol and drug addiction. In *On Writing* he describes the first time he got drunk on a class trip to Washington in 1966 (87–92). When King wrote *The Shining*, he did not recognize himself in the portrait of the alcoholic author, but from his current perspective, he can analyze the various defenses he used to deny his addiction. He never really acknowledged how much he drank until the Maine legislature mandated recycling cans and bottles, and he could actually see how many cans he accumulated in just a few days (94–95). Even though he knew he was an alcoholic by 1975, he had not admitted to it or to the drug addiction that was also a part of his life by 1985. Finally in 1986 Tabitha organized an intervention to demonstrate to her husband the extent of his trouble. She gave him the choice of getting help or losing her and the children. He found that he could still write sober and has remained that way up to the present (*On Writing* 96–99).

King's family has always been central to his life. Unlike many famous couples, he and his wife maintain a strong marriage. Their two sons, Joe and Owen, have followed in their parents' writing careers. Their daughter, Naomi, has become a Universalist minister. King even has a grandchild, Joe's son (Dubner, "Demon" 35). The strong family unit created by his mother continues in King's own life.

The Kings have generously shared the benefits of success. King participates in many national charitable activities, but causes in Maine have benefited the most. The Kings have given money to the University of Maine-Orono swimming and diving programs and the Durham Elementary School for library books. They donated $750,000 in matching funds for the Old Town public library. Old Town, where Tabitha grew up, named a wing of the library in her honor. They also contributed matching funds to the Eastern Maine Medical Center for a pediatrics unit. Perhaps King's most visible contribution to the community is his donation of $1 million for the construction of a 1,500-seat baseball park for Little League and Senior League teams in Bangor. Some residents call it "The Field of Screams" (Beahm, *Stephen King Companion* 189–90).

THE ACCIDENT

The very discipline and determination that shape King's career almost ended it and then made it possible for him to come back. On June 19, 1999, King found that he would just have time to complete the four-mile walk in western Maine that had become part of his daily routine before a planned outing with the family. He had just returned from dropping Owen off at the airport (Dubner, "Demon" 35), and as he walked up a steep hill on Route 5 a van driven by Bryan Smith came over the top and hit him. King was able to turn slightly before the impact so his head did not hit the van's steel support post that would have caused even further damage or death. But he was severely injured in this accident. The driver, Bryan Smith, who had a bad driving record already, including driving under the influence, was not looking at the road because his dog, a rottweiler called Bullet, had distracted him. In order to avoid the possibility of its becoming an object for fans, King purchased the Dodge Caravan that hit him. The driver pled to the lesser of the two offenses charged against him and received a suspended jail sentence and a year without his license (*On Writing* 262).

King credits the emergency response procedures with saving his life. He had to be air-lifted out of the first hospital to another in Lewiston, Maine. His leg was broken in nine places; he had a hip fracture, four broken ribs, and a collapsed lung. The doctor was able to save his leg with multiple surgeries. After three weeks in the hospital King went home on July 9. In addition to physical therapy, he had to have another operation in early August. In the midst of the pain and barely able to sit for any length of time, King knew he had to get back to work. "I had been in terrible situations before which the writing had helped me get over—had helped me forget myself for at least a little while" (*On Writing* 266). Late in July Tabitha set up a place for him to write, and he began work again. While it was hard for him to start once he had he was happy to be back at work. "The scariest moment is always just before you start. After that, things can only get better" (*On Writing* 269). King still had to undergo two more operations and deal with a serious infection. He is once more fully involved with the work he loves. As a result of the accident, he delayed the publication of a novel he had worked on before it occurred. *From a Buick 8* deals with a major automobile accident, and it is now scheduled for release in the spring of 2002. King's readers are relieved that he has recovered from his injuries and is writing again.

While King continues to publish in the traditional way through an established publishing house, he also has challenged this establishment by turning to e-publishing. His first venture into this new technology was the e-novella *Riding the Bullet*, released through Scribners. It shocked the publishing world with its wide distribution as the first e-book that exceeded 500,000 downloads. King had thought there would be 16,000 downloads (Dubner, "Demon" 33). He followed this success with his own release of a novel that had been sitting in a drawer since the eighties, *The Plant*, the story of an author who sends a man-eating plant to a publisher. He placed it on his Web site and relied on an honor system for the payments. While it was somewhat successful, not all of those who downloaded it were honorable. In order to keep King publishing the installments, some fans tried to pay for those who didn't. Claiming the pressure of other obligations, King has temporarily suspended the publication of additional episodes.

FILMS

In *Danse Macabre*, King devotes several chapters to horror films and acknowledges their influence on him and his work. He lists about a hundred fantasy/horror films and indicates his personal favorites. King also readily admits that films of his work have been important in contributing to his success. The film of *Carrie* did much to make people aware of this new author and boosted sales of that novel and *'Salem's Lot*, which followed it. King is not always happy with the film adaptations of his novels. And there are times when the public has agreed. While the quality of cinematic versions of his novels may vary, no film based on a work by King exactly reproduces the original. Films communicate visually, while novels use words and often deal with the thoughts of the characters. Certain elements of the plot work better on paper than on the screen. Watching a film of a King work is never a substitute for reading his fiction.

King has viewed the films based on his novels with varying degrees of approval. While he is interested in what Stanley Kubrick did when he filmed *The Shining*, he feels that he and Kubrick had different opinions of what was important. With *The Lawnmower Man*, he was angry that another story was grafted onto one of his short stories just to use his name. He took the production company to court and got his name removed from the film. King has worked on some of the adaptations of his films, writing scripts, acting, and directing. His first acting experience was in one of the stories in *Creepshow*, an original screenplay of his. The director, George Romero, asked King to play Jordy Verrill in the segment entitled "The Lonesome Death of Jordy Verrill." King had the opportunity to direct his own work with the film *Maximum Overdrive*. While he enjoyed the process, he is not eager to direct another film. He found it to be too much like work, and it took too much time (Underwood and Miller, *Feast of Fear* 261). Recently he published the screenplay of the television miniseries *Storm of the Century* (1999).

Public reception of films adapted from King's work has varied with the quality of the film. Many nonfans have been surprised at some of the films. People associate King with supernatural horror, but Rob Reiner's *Stand By Me*, a moving tale about boys growing up, based on King's story "The Body," found an audience beyond his usual fans. *Misery*,

Reiner's second King film, interested a similar audience and won an Academy Award for its star, Kathy Bates. Reiner named his production company Castle Rock Entertainment, after King's fictional town. Recently *The Shawshank Redemption*, which many feel failed to make money because of its title, also surprised people when they learned that its source was the King story, "Rita Hayworth and the Shawshank Redemption," from *Different Seasons*. This film and *Dolores Claiborne* may have suffered at the box office because they disappointed King fans looking for horror and failed to attract an audience put off by the King connection.

The Green Mile was successfully adapted and generated a certain amount of critical acclaim. The film was nominated for several Academy Awards, including Best Picture. Other novels are currently either being adapted or under consideration for film treatments. The first section of *Hearts in Atlantis*, "Low Men in Yellow Coats," became a film with the same title as the book. It was released in the fall of 2001, and a film of *The Girl Who Loved Tom Gordon* is being developed at the time of this writing. King is also producing his first television series based on the director Lars Von Trier's 1994 mini-series, *The Kingdom*, a story set in a haunted hospital (*Uncut* 13).

King's work has also found its way to television with varying degrees of success. *'Salem's Lot* was an early television adaptation. In the last few years both *The Stand* and *The Langoliers*, published in *Four Past Midnight*, have appeared to bolster network standings during ratings weeks. And *Storm of the Century* was written specially for television. While King remains concerned about how his name is used in adaptations, his works will continue to be adapted as long as there is public interest in them.

KING'S STYLE AND THE FUTURE

While the subjects King deals with in his fiction change, his approach to his writing remains consistent. His style has developed and matured, but he still writes because he has stories he has to tell. He also wants to tell them a certain way. King has always believed in the importance of the story and the characters who inhabit them. "The stories themselves may be unbelievable. But within the framework of the stories I'm concerned that what people do in these stories should be as real as possible and that the characters of the people should be as real as possible" (Underwood and Miller, *Feast of Fear* 232). He reiterates his concern for the real at many points in *On Writing*. King understands the difference between writing fiction and remaining true to the way ordinary people think and react. King concentrates on what he knows and has experienced, and finds it difficult to write about something outside of his experience. For example, he found it hard to write a scene in *Cujo* where a couple discusses the affair the wife is having (Underwood and Miller, *Feast of Fear* 234–35). But King also believes that he must do difficult things to maintain his artistic integrity. At the same time he is aware that his strength comes from working within his own experience. "The people who I write about are generally speaking not very rich or very cultured, maybe because I'm not very cultured, because I don't have any idea what it is to be rich . . . like estates in Newport . . . or having portraits in the hall" (Underwood and Miller, *Feast of Fear* 235–36).

King retains his fears of the monsters that may live under the bed but includes fewer of them in his recent work. His most recent novels exhibit a conflict between opposing forces in his work that is becoming more and more pronounced. King wants the kind of serious consideration awarded to non-genre authors, but he cannot resist the pull of those forms that have been at the center of his work for so long. *Cujo* and *The Girl Who Loved Tom Gordon* deal with realistic horror. *Rose Madder* (1995) employs the supernatural in a traditional manner but one King has not previously used. *Dolores Claiborne*, aside from brief telepathic moments, is a realistic novel. *Insomnia* has interesting connections with the Dark Tower series. *Desperation* and *The Regulators* use the same characters in very different situations. As Stephen J. Dubner says of *Hearts in Atlantis* and *Bag of Bones*: "They are big, serious-ish books. . . . But by story's end the ghosts have arrived. A reader feels almost as if the writer wanted to resist but couldn't" (34). King wants to interest readers who would not usually read fiction associated with his name, but he is still drawn to horror and science fiction and still pleases those fans who have set expectations of his work.

Because his children are grown, he finds himself less interested in childhood, and he has dealt with more mature adults in most of his recent fiction. Certain projects continue to develop themes he began to explore in his college days. The Dark Tower is an ongoing series, and its themes also appear in novels like *Insomnia* and *Rose Madder* and in *Hearts in Atlantis*. He is also dealing more frequently with themes that have been a smaller part of his early work, such as aging and wife and child abuse. The friends in *Dreamcatcher* are far from the young protagonists of his early fiction. One character is so tired of his life that he would like to end it. *Hearts in Atlantis* starts with a young boy, but it too ends up with older men who fight to keep going in the midst of the mistakes they have made in their lives.

This interest in adults has led to an exploration of issues of masculinity only suggested in his earlier fiction. King is now concerned with assessing the nature of the hero in modern society. While the Dark Tower series presents traditional views of the stranger or the group of strangers who ride into town and attempt to save the world, many of his later novels concern surviving with some remnant of honor and dignity. Characters realize that heroism is sometimes a matter of being in the right place at the right time and being able to make the right choice. The young in King's fiction often act without thinking because they do not realize or fear the possible consequences of their actions. His older characters must live with what they have done.

In addition to theme and character, King has expanded his interest in the structure of the work. He turned to the serial publication of a novel with *The Green Mile*. *Hearts in Atlantis* tracks characters and themes through fiction of varying length from novella to short story. With *Desperation* and *The Regulators* he creates two books that share elements of character, plot, and setting. He has also experimented with different kinds of e-publication, from the novella to another serial publication, *The Plant*. The sequel to his collaboration with Peter Straub, *The Talisman*, was published in the fall of 2001. *Black House*, as it is called, answers questions about the Dark Tower series and its connection to *Hearts in Atlantis*.

All of these works are examples of the way King continues to explore and enlarge his fictional world. He does not know how his work will stand up in the future. He thinks it will still be in libraries if we still have libraries. He knows the test of a writer is how long his work is around after his death. "After I'm dead some eleven year old kid will be going along through the stacks the way I went through the library stacks and discovered Richard Matheson and Algernon Blackwood, and he'll find this dusty book and he'll take it home and he'll lose an afternoon" (Underwood and Miller, *Feast of Fear* 238). Charles Dickens was the most popular writer of his time. Now he is a classroom assignment. King's view of his future is a little more hopeful. Maybe it's better to be picked off a shelf by chance than to be assigned in an English class. However, King is now assigned in some classes as teachers appreciate the fact that assigning King is one way to get their students to enjoy reading.

Everyone who reads King's work has favorites. While I like some of his novels better than others, I have presented some of his most recent fiction in this edition of this book. With *Bag of Bones* King changed publishers and some people sensed a new seriousness in his fiction. While

Desperation, The Regulators, and *The Green Mile* predate this shift, they are examples of his ongoing experimentation with narrative form. *Wizard and Glass* is the most recent novel in the extended series dealing with the Dark Tower. Some readers may miss the kind of horror King became famous for in his earlier fiction. But his most recent works demonstrate an ever increasing mastery of his craft. I also attempted to select works that are representative of the various avenues that King has pursued in his writing from his experiments with form, his use of a pseudonym, and his creation of a series with a fictional world that extends over much of his work to those works that attempt to expand the themes of his craft.

2

Genre

WHAT IS A GENRE?

Readers of popular fiction often make selections based on previous experiences with works they have enjoyed. One way to group literature is by genre. In a bookstore, readers expect the mystery shelves to contain books dealing with crimes and their solutions. The section on romance will present books that concentrate on love relationships. The science fiction section contains books dealing with speculative fiction that may or may not actually take place in the future. The separation of fiction into different genres is a way of focusing the reader's expectations and the author's creativity. The categories allow readers to select literature they like and avoid categories they may not. These categories also fulfill certain expectations and influence the reader's interaction with the work. If someone does not like the fright and tension generated by horror fiction, she or he can avoid that section of the bookstore. Similarly, authors may be interested in dealing with a certain way of looking at the world. If they like to create alternate universes, they might choose to write in the fantasy or science fiction genre. If they like a world where order is restored, the good are rewarded, and the bad are punished they might favor the endings produced in traditional mystery novels. Readers of suspense novels also like tension, but they expect events that could happen in their world, unlike the supernatural in the world of horror.

Works of nonfiction can also be categorized by genre. History and biography are examples of nonfiction genres. Fiction and nonfiction are opposites and generally deal with their subjects in different ways. For example, biography concentrates on the life of a person, and history deals with public events. Readers of these genres have different expectations than readers of fiction. They want accurate facts about events or personal revelations about people. Fiction may concentrate on people or events, but it need not rely on actual facts to tell its story. The divisions among fictional genres such as horror, fantasy, and science fiction are less clear than those between fiction and nonfiction. Although readers and authors may not always agree on where to place a book, they agree that the categories do exist. People who don't read horror novels may say, "I don't read that kind of book," and be able to give reasons why they don't like the genre.

Readers may disagree about which works belong in each category because genres do not remain static. Genres develop over time, reflecting shifts in literary styles and tastes. Genres reflect the society around them, but they do more than mirror the world. They may show us our fears about our lives and about both our personal future and the future of the planet. Each uses narrative, motive, setting, characterization, and symbolism to create its own fictional world. Distinct elements can provide easy ways to determine genres. Consider, for example, a story with a western setting that takes place in the future. If setting is the most important aspect of the genre, readers might characterize it as a western rather than science fiction. The author, however, might think that the time frame is more important and call it science fiction. No definitive list of the basics of a genre exists, but readers and authors can describe the elements that characterize it. Much of the pleasure in experiencing a genre comes from the anticipation of meeting the familiar and expected in a new form.

In addition to generating feelings specific to their genre, such works may also be organized to tell the story in a way that reflects their category. Readers of mysteries expect solutions at the end of the novel, but a work of horror may have a more open ending suggesting that the evil has not been completely contained. Novels printed in a serial format or in a series of connected novels may conclude each section with a suspenseful open ending to make certain the reader continues to follow the serial or series. Readers who do not like this kind of format might avoid novels organized in this way. At the same time, authors may enjoy dealing with the same characters over a longer period of time.

WHAT IS THE HORROR GENRE?

Most people think of Stephen King as someone who writes horror fiction even though, as the end of this chapter indicates, he is associated with other genres. King does, however, remain primarily associated with this genre, and before any exploration of his specific approach to his use of other genres can be explored, the components of horror need to be defined and understood to better appreciate his contributions. Some authors and critics are interested in the way horror relates to its audience. Most people read horror fiction or see horror films because they like the kinds of reactions this genre stimulates in them. King wants the reader to be scared by his work. Some read horror fiction as a way of self-testing, an experience of the fear of death without dying. Some critics see it as being similar to getting on the most frightening ride in the amusement park. Readers can see how brave they are without actually risking our lives.

Many people define horror by its central characters. Such creatures as Dr. Frankenstein's creation, Dracula, and the wolfman are the typical monsters in the horror genre. Each one of these creatures has a history and has developed over a period of time. But horror covers more than just works dealing with monsters. Most readers can make long lists of the kinds of creatures identified with horror, especially in films, and in literature where there are psychotic slashers and men with chainsaws. But such a list would also demonstrate that not all monsters are alike and not all horror deals with monsters. The character approach is not the clearest way to define this genre.

Some students of this genre find that the best way to examine it is to deal with the way horror fiction is organized or structured. Examining the organization of a horror story shows that it shares certain traits with other types of fiction. Horror stories share with many other kinds of literature the use of suspense as a tactic. The tension experienced when a character goes into the attic, down into the basement, or just into the abandoned house is partially a result of suspense. The reader doesn't know what is going to happen. But that suspense is intensified through knowledge of the genre. Previous experience tells the reader that characters involved in the world of horror always meet something awful when they go where they shouldn't. Part of the tension is created because they are doing something where trouble is the expected result. In *The Regulators*, Tak gives form to the horrible changes in the neighborhood through experiences with popular culture on television. Stephen King refers directly to our anticipation of horror. In *'Salem's Lot* Susan approaches the house that is the source of evil. "She found herself thinking of those drive-in horror movie epics where the heroine goes venturing up the narrow attic stairs . . . or down into some dark, cobwebby cellar . . . and she . . . thinking: *What a silly bitch . . . I'd never do that!*" (260). Of course Susan's fears are justified. She does end up dead in the basement, a victim of the vampire.

If the horror genre uses the character's search for information to create suspense, it controls when and where knowledge becomes available. Because the reader remains outside of the situation she or he usually knows more than the characters. Advance knowledge creates suspense because the reader can anticipate what is going to happen. The author can play with those expectations by either confirming them or surprising the audience with a different outcome. When suspense is an important element in fiction, the plot is often the most critical part of the story. Readers care more about what happens next than about who the characters are or where the story is set. Horror stories usually have a point when the source of the horror is explained through references to supernatural events that are presented as factual occurrences. But setting is often considered a part of the horror genre. If the genre has traditional monsters, it also has traditional settings. Only authors who want to challenge the tradition place events in bright, beautiful parks. Readers expect a connection between the setting and the events in this genre. They are not surprised to find old houses, abandoned castles, damp cellars, or dark forests as important elements in the horror story.

Some people make further distinctions based on how the stories are organized. Critics can divide stories into different categories based on how the reader comes to believe in the events related and how they are explained. Stories that deal with parallel worlds expect the acceptance of those worlds without question. Readers and viewers just believe Dorothy is in Oz; they accept Oz as a parallel world separate from their own. Other times events seem to be supernatural but turn out to have natural explanations: the ghosts turn out to be squirrels in the attic, or things that move mysteriously are part of a plot to drive someone crazy. Sometimes the supernatural is the result of the way the central character sees the world, as in stories told from the point of view of a crazy person. But at times readers are not sure and hesitate about believing in the possibility of the supernatural. When I first read *Dracula* I seriously considered hanging garlic on my windows because I believed that vampires could exist. This type of hesitation, when readers almost believe, falls into the general category of the "fantastic" (Todorov, *The Fantastic* 25). Often horror has its greatest effect because its audience almost believes, or temporarily believes while reading the book or watching the film, that the events are possible.

Yet another way of categorizing works of horror is by the source of the horror. Some horror comes from inside the characters. Something goes wrong inside, and a person turns into a monster. Dr. Frankenstein's need for knowledge turns him into the kind of person who creates a monster. Dr. Jekyll also values his desire for information above all else and creates Mr. Hyde. In another kind of horror story the threat to the central character or characters comes from outside. An outside force may invade the character and then force the evil out again. The vampire attacks the victim, but then the victim becomes a vampire and attacks others. Stories of ghosts or demonic possession also fall into this category.

Critics can also look at the kinds of themes common to horror. Many works concentrate on the conflict between good and evil. Common assumptions about these categories may be tested in the genre. Progress is not always viewed as positive. New technologies bring negative possibilities. Robots work for or against their creators and represent attitudes toward those who are different in society. Works about the fantastic may deal with the search for forbidden knowledge that appears in much horror literature. Such quests are used as a way of examining attitudes toward knowledge. While society may believe that new knowledge is always good, the horror genre may question this assumption, examining how such advances affect the individual and society.

Modern horror fiction begins with Gothic fiction. Horace Walpole's *The Castle of Otranto* (1764) is considered the first real Gothic novel, the first of many to deal with heroines in jeopardy, rotting castles and monasteries, and natural and supernatural events combined to create sensational suspense. Much of the supernatural threat comes from outside the character. At this period people were just beginning to question the relationship between the world of science and the world of religion. Scientific advances gave rational explanations for many events previously thought to have supernatural or religious sources. This conflict between the world of science and the world of belief is reflected in Gothic literature as it developed over the eighteenth and nineteenth centuries. The story of Dr. Frankenstein's experiments to create life reflects society's concerns with the role of science. The Gothic novel generally reflects concerns about advances in knowledge and whether they will be good or bad for society.

As the horror genre developed, the idea of threats from the inside grew. For many people religion lost its power as a source of supernatural events. Horror had to be believable within a world where more and more could be explained rationally. While the genre still kept its connection to the more general concerns of society, the source of the horror was more personal. In King's *Christine*, for example, the car turns into a destructive monster because it is bought and restored by a teenager who fails to fit into his social group. Religion, too, has lost much of its power in this novel. The car is destroyed without the use of religious objects. But the modern horror novel is still concerned with the search for knowledge and how it affects our world. Modern science and technology are often sources for evil. In *Firestarter*, a child's powers are the result of scientific experiments on her parents. Readers might even think of science as a substitute for religion in many modern horror stories. In the Gothic story, we accept devils and evil monks as integral parts of the world of the priests, crosses, and holy water by means of which the evil is destroyed. Now people believe in the power of science to create the new monsters of modern horror and also to help us control them. Additional sources of horror can come from the internal conflicts in a society. Clashes between two races create the ghosts that haunt *Bag of Bones*. In modern society, belief in horror does not diminish, but new sources for it emerge.

KING'S VIEW OF THE WRITING PROCESS

Before moving to an appreciation of King's approach to various genres, it is interesting to survey his view of fiction writing in general. In his book *On Writing*, he presents a detailed analysis of both how he writes and how he thinks others should approach the task. For King writing is a serious business. He sees it as a form of telepathy, a contact between his mind and that of the reader (106–7). Writing is also a craft that requires practice and the correct use of the correct tools. In this book King details both the tools and the process with examples from his own work.

In the section called "Toolbox," King uses the analogy of his grandfather's toolbox as a container for the basic necessities for the writer: vocabulary, elements of style, and good habits. He moves from such specifics as the avoidance of passive voice and adverbs (122–24) to paragraph construction (134). While King does suggest that the good writer must adhere to totally correct grammatical constructions at all times, he advocates the use of such elements as sentence fragments to help the pace and flow of the language (133). He illustrates all of his ideas with examples from both his work and that of others.

The introduction of examples from other authors underlines one of King's basic views of how the writer learns the craft: reading other works in the genre. In the section titled "On Writing," King presents the larger elements necessary for fiction: narration, description, and dialogue (163). He also deals with character and plot. But he feels that his stories come out of situation and character. (164). He makes a distinction between plotted novels and situational novels. King uses "situation" the way this book presents "plot." He uses "plot" for those novels that are more schematic, where the story has a certain direction before the novel begins and there is no deviation from that plan, as opposed to those works where the characters seem to lead the story in certain directions. King states that *Rose Madder* and *Insomnia* are plotted works, while *Bag of Bones* may seem plotted but is really a situational work (169). For King close observation of the real world is the key to creating good dialogue, description, and characters. The writer must be in contact with others and be true to their experiences (178–89). Characters, like people in the outside world, grow and change (190). Through all of his presentation of what makes a good writer, King constantly emphasizes the necessity for truth. Even though situations may come from the writer's imagination, people and places must reflect the experiences of the reader and the author.

King ends his presentation of the writing process with a detailed description of how he revises his work. In addition to correcting errors, he uses his two revisions and final polish to address concerns about symbolism and theme (197). He uses examples from his novels to detail how he develops a theme and then presents his major themes as he sees them in his work.

> These deep interests . . . include how difficult it is . . . to close Pandora's technobox once it's open (*The Stand, The Tommyknockers, Firestarter*); the question of why, if there is a God, such terrible things happen (*The Stand, Desperation, The Green Mile*); the thin line between reality and fantasy (*The Dark Half, Bag of Bones, The Drawing of the Three*); and most of all, the terrible attraction violence sometimes has for fundamentally good people (*The Shining, The Dark Half*). (207)

King also acknowledges the recurring exploration of the relationships between children and adults and "the healing power of the human imagination" (207). His analysis demonstrates how central many of King's thematic concerns are to his connection to popular fiction and especially the horror genre with its emphasis of the workings of evil in the world.

KING'S VIEW OF THE HORROR GENRE

King describes his view of the genre and lists his favorite literature and film in *Danse Macabre* (1981). He presents his view on the writing of works in the genre in *On Writing*. A critic, Tony Magistrale, analyzes the points King makes about modern horror in this work (*Stephen King, The Second Decade* 21–24). All of his points deal with the reader's relationship with modern horror media, including film and television as well as literature. Magistrale's first point is that horror *"allows us to prove our bravery"* (22). Many people see this as an important element in the genre. Readers can test themselves without really facing physical danger. They can assure themselves that they might respond heroically in the same situation, or they can face their fears by continuing to read, even though they are frightened. King relates these experiences to teenagers' love of the horror genre and the amusement park. People who hold their hands in the air on the roller coaster are testing their bravery in the same way people do when they read a scary story or watch a frightening film.

Second, says Magistrate, horror *"enables us to reestablish feelings of normality"* (22). Horror allows readers to see that their own world is not as bad as the world of the novel. They may not like school, but their lives are certainly better than those of the central characters in *Carrie*, *Dreamcatcher*, or *Hearts in Atlantis*. Readers may miss dead loved ones, but they have not come back like the family in *Bag of Bones*. Childhoods may have been unhappy, but not all of the readers have lost family members to real or metaphorical monsters, as occurred in *The Regulators*. And our insomnia is nothing compared to the sleeplessness of the characters in the book of that title.

Magistrale's third point may become less valid as King's work develops: *"It confirms our good feelings about the status quo"* (22). King suggests that the horror genre appeals to the conservative because it shows people how bad things might be. The other worlds of the horror novel make readers think their own world isn't that bad. But many of King's recent novels show worlds that are very close to our own. The young girl in *The Girl Who Loved Tom Gordon* steps off the path on a hike with her family into a world filled with very real terror. The friends in *Dreamcatcher* are faced with decisions that lead to heroism. A young boy in *Hearts in Atlantis* suddenly comes in contact with unimagined evil in his town. The reader can see that these problems exist in her or his own world.

His fourth point may suggest why King may be moving toward novels that give the readers ways to deal with social problems: *"It lets us feel we are part of the larger whole"* (22). In *It* we identify with the group that has come together to finally destroy the horror that has been a part of the town for a long time. King returns to a similar group in *Dreamcatcher*. In *The Stand* King examines the benefits and risks of forming groups. He also looks at the family as a group and usually feels that we are better off with groups we form on our own. The people who band together in *Dreamcatcher* promote traditional family values even to the introduction of religion in the novel. The isolation of the neighborhood in *The Regulators* is part of the horror.

Magistrale's fifth point is central to the horror genre: *"It provides an opportunity to penetrate the mystery of death"* (22). Readers don't often deal with concerns about death in everyday life. A novel like *Pet Sematary* shows one way of coping with the death of loved ones. Readers also get some sense of possible versions of life after death in this novel, *It*, and *The Tommyknockers*. People can also identify with a character who is trying to avoid death. In *Cujo* a mother is trapped in her car with her child and has to face the possibility of death from a rabid dog. Facing death goes beyond just testing our bravery. The young boy in *The Cycle of the Werewolf* is willing to sacrifice to rid his town of the murderer. Horror may even suggest what might happen beyond death. The ghosts that haunt *Bag of Bones* must be pacified through the revelation of the causes of their deaths. Readers also see how characters may be willing to die to save others in such novels as *Desperation*. Even the death and destruction of Vietnam are confronted in *Hearts in Atlantis*, where characters feel that their experiences in that conflict penetrate the mystery of death. The movement through various time periods in the Tower series challenges traditional images of death. Characters who seem to be dead reappear. Others seem to live through events that would encompass many ordinary lifetimes.

If death is a major focus of the horror genre, his sixth point connects fears to a larger concern: *"It permits us to indulge our darkest collective and social anxieties"* (23). The genre gives us ways to deal with some fears about the world. In *The Dead Zone* the central character's powers give him knowledge about destructive political forces. Both *Carrie* and *Dreamcatcher* examine concerns about what happens to the outsider in high school. Readers can then go deeper, to a subtext that connects the world of high school to society as a whole. The genre gives people ways of examining the larger problems facing society—such as the racism depicted in *Bag of Bones*. This concept also connects to the earlier points about the way the genre deals with the effects of science and technology on our lives.

The seventh point is a major element in many of King's novels: *"It lets us return to childhood"* (23). Often children provide the key to an understanding of the world of horror. They see clearly because they have not yet learned the adult habits of disbelief. Adults must return to their childhood if they are to survive in King's world of horror. Or they must finally confront their childhood terrors. Parents are usually trying too hard to be adults to be able to connect with their children and accept their view of the world. Only the exceptional adult who has not totally lost contact with the world of childhood can see into the horror in King's novels. Children do not have to be convinced; they believe what they see. They also have an innocence and goodness often lost in the adult. The characters in *It* confront the evil twice. The first time they succeed because they are children. The second time, as adults, they must confront their childhood fears in order to finally conquer the horror. Many of King's adults can defeat the evils in the genre only after they deal with their childhood fears. To survive, the heroine of *Gerald's Game* must deal with the moment of child abuse she experienced. In *Dreamcatcher* King expands on the emotions generating these fears by distinguishing between a child's view of the world and that of the adult. Many adults have seen too much or experienced too much. Their lives are damaged. The adults in *Hearts in Atlantis* share experiences in Vietnam with others. A return to the innocence of childhood is no longer possible. Many of the elements of the horror genre come from childhood fears. The horrible things that can happen in the dark, terrifying strangers, the monsters who live in the closet and under the bed are all elements of the genre. People return to the world of childhood when they accept the possibility that these things may still exist. Those with enough imagination to get up and close the closet door so that they can sleep are still close to childhood. Such characters are the ones who most often deal with evil in King's world and, as readers, are the ones who respond to this world. In his recent fiction King shows how difficult it is to retain the values of childhood as people leave that period in their lives.

The final point in Magistrale's list returns the reader to the everyday world: *"It enables us to transcend the world of darkness and negation"* (23). King suggests that readers leave their experience of the genre with skills that allow them to cope with the evil they find in their own lives. As readers identify with those who are tested, they see what is important for their own survival. They learn that they must confront fears and believe in the power of good. King also suggests that such belief becomes more difficult as a person gets older. Readers can also see that their problems are not that difficult when they watch characters master much greater ones. Horror also allows readers to return temporarily to the world of childhood through identification with fictional characters. If readers regain its fears, they also regain its beliefs.

Many people think that an interest in horror is unhealthy. They see the monsters, the evil, and the darkness. King wants people to realize that the genre moves us through horror to a world where basic human values have been tested and reaffirmed. The world at the end of his novels is not the same as at the beginning. Towns may be destroyed, some people may have died, but others have been tested and have survived. The few who do succeed in overcoming evil face a world that has been cleansed. We have hope for our own world. Whatever may happen, good can win, and we have learned how to work toward the defeat of evil in our own world.

OTHER GENRES IN KING'S FICTION

Readers tend to think of King as a writer of horror fiction, but not all of his work falls directly into this category. Some combine horror with other genres. *Carrie* is set a few years in the future, but people read it as a horror novel. The setting is only a way of making the story more real. If the reader hasn't heard of Carrie's powers, it is because the story hasn't happened yet. Other novels are clearly part of other genres. In recent fiction, King has experimented with the divisions between genres. At times he moves outside of traditional genre formats entirely in an effort to move into a more mainstream literary format.

Suspense Fiction

The suspense genre shares much of its structure with horror. The hesitation between belief and disbelief in the supernatural that forms the horror genre is transformed into a fear of the real in this genre. Suspense also has connections to the mystery story. All encourage identification with the central character or characters. And all use the plot and the reader's expectations to create tension. Mystery adds the puzzle of the question of identification of crime and criminal. If readers know more than the characters, they can anticipate what might happen. If they share the viewpoint of the character, they identify with that character. While in horror the source of the tension may be supernatural, in suspense its source is the natural world. In *Misery* an author is trapped in the house of his biggest fan. Readers identify with him and his attempts to escape and outwit his captor. The woman who has trapped him may be crazy, but there are natural causes for her mental state. In *Gerald's Game* a woman is trapped. A visitor seems to be supernatural, but readers find out that he too has a natural origin. *Cujo* is a real dog who suffers from rabies. Patricia McFarland in *The Girl Who Loved Tom Gordon* must face terrors from the real world when she gets lost in the woods. Her problems in surviving this ordeal provide the suspense. In these works King demonstrates that terror can have its source in our everyday world.

In other novels King gives logical reasons for events that appear to have supernatural causes. In *The Dead Zone* and *Firestarter*, characters' powers have logical origins. Such things could but have not happened in the everyday world of the reader's experience. *The Green Mile* combines natural and supernatural events with suspense and mystery in a structure that generates its own tension. The serial format of this novel means that each section ends at a moment that leaves the reader in excited anticipation for the next. At the same time the story examines the mystery of the true identity of the killer of the two girls. Paul Edgecombe takes on the role of detective when he discovers the real killer. The events in the prison and John Coffey's powers may have supernatural connections, but some may believe in healing powers of special people—a belief that gives the fantastic events a religious and miraculous overtone. Readers already know some events in suspense novels to be possible: people have been attacked by rabid dogs or crazy fans. But other events require them to accept the unlikely: they do not know of people who have healed others with their minds. In the suspense genre the most important factor is the effect of the story on the audience. While elements of other genres may permeate the fiction, the tone and structure of the work lead the reader to anticipate future events—both waiting for and dreading the next page of the novel.

Science Fiction

Most people think science fiction explores events in the future where the characters face problems in worlds beyond the experience of the reader. But the term *speculative fiction* that is also applied to the genre does not necessarily demand a setting in the future. It may even explore actions happening right now in parallel worlds. Science fiction may deal with problems created by events that have not yet occurred. *The Stand* examines the difficulties facing the survivors of a strange epidemic. The central characters in *The Tommyknockers* uncover an alien spacecraft. As the craft is revealed, strange things happen to people near it. *Dreamcatcher*, set in the near future, explores a more widespread contact with an alien life form. The Dark Tower series also deals with an unspecified future. In these novels characters travel in time, another trait of the science fiction genre. Science fiction creates uncertainty just as horror and suspense do. But in this genre, readers are interested in how events work out in the future or in other worlds.

Science fiction uses myths and symbols to help create its world, and its picture of the future may be critical of the present. Authors may deal with the impact of technology or social structures on characters and may use a future or alternate universe as a means of criticizing contemporary society. For example, *The Talisman*, which King wrote with Peter Straub, deals with concern about the effects of nuclear power on our future. *Dreamcatcher* deals with an alien invasion that may have already happened by the time a reader opens the book. It criticizes the more extreme reactions of the military to the threat posed by the aliens.

Fantasy

The fantasy genre is closely related to both horror and science fiction. Fantasy explores supernatural events. But these events do not happen in the reader's world, and the author does not try to make them seem realistic. Fantasy literature is usually set in an alternate parallel world in a mythical past. Fantasy also shares certain traits with the fairy tale. Fairy tales occur in a mythical world and focus on supernatural or magical events. Many of King's novels have connections to popular fairy tales. The prom's "crowning queen" sequence at the end of *Carrie* recalls elements of Cinderella. Jack in *The Shining* becomes Bluebeard. Children, who are so important in King's horror fiction, are the intended audience for fairy tales. Like science fiction, fantasy explores parallel or alternate worlds. While science fiction may deal with alien universes, fantasy locates its world in a different reality that is still connected to the reader's planet. Some of the stories that form *Hearts in Atlantis* have strong connections to this genre. "Blind Willie" and "Why We're in Vietnam" are set in a known world, but the events contain elements that could not actually happen.

The Eyes of the Dragon is King's major exploration of the fantasy genre. He wrote the book for his daughter because she didn't like horror. This novel deals with two brothers, an evil wizard, and magical events. Even the illustrations add to the fantasy and the sense of an undefined past.

The opening page looks like an illuminated manuscript, and each chapter begins with a letter in a special typeface. Even though there is much tension in the story, readers are drawn along by events the way they might be in a fairy tale. And even though terrible things may happen, readers know that the fairy tale must have a happy ending. They have faith that good magic will win over bad. But even in this novel there is a hint of evil that goes beyond the boundaries of any genre. Evil in this novel is represented by a man called Flagg. Flagg reappears in other forms in other King novels and as himself in *The Stand*. In King's world, where religion is sometimes no longer a power, Flagg becomes a kind of Satan, an evil figure who escapes to reappear later in another world or with another name. "Flagg always showed up with a different face and a different bag of tricks, but two things about him were always the same. He always came hooded, a man who seemed almost to have no face, and he never came as the King himself, but always as the whisperer in the shadows, the man who poured poison into the porches of the Kings' ears" (*Eyes* 62).

King's use of Flagg is just one element that unites his work. This character also appears in the Dark Tower series' novels like *Wizard and Glass*. These novels provide the main focus for a theory of human relationships and destiny that pervades many of King's novels outside of this series. The characters are part of a group united by the goal of finding the Dark Tower and saving the world. Even though King's main emphasis is on the horror genre, his themes are remarkably consistent.

Recent Works and Genre Fiction

King tends more and more to cross traditional genre boundaries by creating worlds that exist in more than one work and genre. All genres exist as elements of popular culture. King's work both reflects and creates this culture. He has always reflected the everyday life of his readers in the world of his characters from a Walkman to a plastic model of a monster. King takes this inclusion of popular culture a step further when he treats his own creations as though they existed in the real world. Characters in his novels read the *Misery* series or see as history events that occurred in the fictional town of Derry. By including elements from one novel in another King unites his fictional world and blends genres.

The Dark Tower series takes this melding of elements of fantasy, western, and horror genres further by including types of fiction not usually found in King. At the same time it creates a universe that permeates many of King's other works. The Dark Tower represents an enduring human quest at the same time that the image of the tower and the theme of the quest are strong parts of traditional fantasy literature. King expands the use of these elements to novels where the horror is grounded in reality such as *Insomnia* and *Hearts in Atlantis*. The image of the Dark Tower appears in both. In *Insomnia*, King connects it to classical images of the operation of fate. In *Hearts in Atlantis*, Ted Brautigan is directly involved in the ongoing conflict to reach the tower. King promises that some of the questions raised by Ted in "Low Men in Yellow Coats" in the latter work will be answered in the forthcoming sequel to *The Talisman*, *Black House*. For both of these works the Dark Tower exists as a force beneath the surface of the text, introducing elements of the fantasy genre where no one would expect to find them.

In addition to the quest motif, the Dark Tower series examines the role of the individual in relation to the group and the conflict between destiny and free will. The shifting genres and time frames of the novels in the series suggest a pattern that shapes the characters' lives. When Roland relates a story from his past, readers know that he survives because he is telling it. The genre form itself presents a set of expectations in the reader that can also be connected to destiny. In a horror work they expect the evil to be destroyed by the good. Readers assume the murderer will be caught in that genre. Novels such as *Desperation* and *Dreamcatcher* combine horror with an examination of the role of free will and move beyond the usual expectations of the genre. In these works the conflict between good and evil extends the usual genre conflicts between monsters and men to concerns about the nature of good and evil. These works deal directly with the choices people make and how they reverberate through their lives and the lives of others.

Recently it seems that King deliberately ventures beyond traditional definitions of genres because his characters and themes demand this expanded vision. Religion and its role in the life of his characters are much more important in *Desperation*. He examines the nature of the traditional genre hero with Roland, gives Johnny Marinville two chances to be a hero in *Desperation* and *The Regulators*, and shows how ordinary people can make decisions that turn them into heroes in *Dreamcatcher*. The combination of genres he employs in recent works actually seems to move them beyond the usual formulas to a fictional world outside of this tradition.

In addition to his expansion of themes in recent works, King also explores different ways to organize his fiction. He has always been concerned with the formal structure of his works, but his ventures into serial publication, e-publication, and a combination of story forms in a single work are indications of his further attempts to develop different ways of presenting genre fiction. Both *The Green Mile* and the e-published *The Plant* are serial novels originally appearing in segments. Readers could read only a part of the story as it was published. Of course King has been involved with the production of a series of novels that appear sporadically and continue the same story in the Dark Tower series, but these other books deal with the serialization of a single work. In *Hearts in Atlantis* he combines novellas and short stories containing some of the same characters and events. Not everything in each story is connected, but the various parts become a whole dealing with the response of several characters to events surrounding the war in Vietnam. With *Desperation* and *The Regulators* he also connects events and characters. This time he uses two different novels to present two versions of the effects on the town's community of re-opening a mine. In all of these examples King demonstrates an ongoing interest in stretching the boundaries of traditional genres and exploring the connections between genre and non-genre fiction.

3

Desperation and *The Regulators* (1996)

In 1996 Stephen King published two companion novels—*Desperation* under his own name and *The Regulators* under his alias, Richard Bachman. As King had already killed off his alter ego in 1985, the opening of the latter suggests that Bachman's widow found this book when moving in 1994. While many of King's works share a common world-view and a vocabulary to express it, especially the Dark Tower series, *Insomnia*, and *Hearts in Atlantis*, these two novels share characters, locations, and even a common source for the evil that is the focus of their plots. The novels even share cover art; the back of each novel contains an image from the other. Yet each also retains the characteristics of its titular author. *Desperation* is longer and less graphically violent than *The Regulators*, and its theme examines the nature of good and evil with greater depth.

A comparison of the two demonstrates the extent to which King has been able to create and maintain the fiction of his alter ego, Richard Bachman. As King indicates on his Web site, he created the fictional author to be able to publish some early works, but the author gradually developed a life of his own. In *The Dark Half*, King deals with such a situation between author and pseudonym and the problems it can generate. For King, the Bachman name became an outlet for his prolific writing without oversaturating the market with King works. He was able to maintain the secrecy of the connection between him and Bachman for quite a while. *Desperation* and *The Regulators* appeared after the connection between the two names was well known. In this case King uses the fiction of the other author with his own life and style as a means of exploring the same idea from two different perspectives. He also can deal in depth with another version of evil in the world and provide his fans with the pleasure of making connections between the two works.

In a sense the two novels are mirror images of each other. They both focus on the family, the nature of sacrifice, the relationship between good and evil, and the role of the group. But they differ in the way that these elements are treated and in the settings in which the stories are placed. Tak, the evil force in both works, emerges from the same mine outside of Desperation, Nevada, but its interaction with humans differs in each novel. In *Desperation* Tak enters and destroys the bodies of various adults both in the community and outside of it. Its evil is countered by the religious beliefs of a young boy. Another young boy is the host for Tak in *The Regulators,* and as a result of this conjunction, it manifests itself in a more childlike manner. The town of Desperation is the setting for the novel of that name. The location of this town in the western United States represents one aspect of the "American Dream": the possibilities represented by open spaces where capitalism clashes with a concern for preserving the environment. *The Regulators* focuses on one street in the town of Wentworth, Ohio, which makes it more of an urban novel, although other locations are also included. King presents Wentworth as a typical town in a region that seems to be most representative of the modern American individual's dream of owning a house, having a family, and enjoying the elements of popular culture so prevalent in this kind of location. The quotations that open each novel further define their complex relationship. *Desperation* opens with a quotation from Salman Rushdie's *The Satanic Verses.* He is an author who has had to deal with religious problems in his own life when Islamic Fundamentalists threatened to kill him because of his depiction of that religion in his book. The quotation deals with a quality of poetry as it relates to the desert. Rather than a standard dedication, *The Regulators'* quotation makes reference to two legendary shadows, the author Jim Thompson and the film director Sam Peckinpah—both associated with popular genres. The film *The Magnificent Seven* is the source of this book's opening quotation, the statement "Mister, we deal in lead," spoken by Steve McQueen (13). The first quotation deals with a man who faced persecution for his writing; the second foregrounds popular culture icons known for the violence of their fictional worlds. Even though there are differences between them, both novels begin with an ordinary everyday world where things go very wrong.

PLOT DEVELOPMENT

In *Desperation* the sense that the ordinary can soon turn into the extraordinary occurs more quickly than in *The Regulators*. Both open with events in the small town in Nevada off Highway 50. *Desperation* is the more complexly structured of the two and the longer novel. It is also the one in which suspense is generated by keeping information from the reader. Events move more rapidly in *The Regulators*, and the reader can often put together pieces of information ahead of the explanation. In the first novel the reader in encouraged to think and in the second to react.

Desperation

This novel is divided into five major parts, each with its own title, and then further segmented into chapters and subchapters. The chapter and subchapter divisions help organize the action and characters. At many times events occur simultaneously in different locations. The smaller segments allow King to indicate when such shifts occur. The first part establishes the basic elements of the novel and brings all of the major characters together. While the collecting of people seems to be random, we gradually learn that there is a purpose to what is happening. In *Desperation*, King provides clues to the events and reasons for characters' actions, but he deliberately provides the characters with information before the reader to generate a constant state of suspense throughout the novel. The reader's role is to try to put together the clues provided by the characters, but the solutions to questions raised are always delayed.

The novel opens with what seems to be a series of routine traffic stops by a policeman. We share the concern of the characters, their relief at what seems to be a simple reason for the policeman to pull them over, and then a growing sense of unease as the situation turns more ominous. In the first case, a couple is driving the husband's sister's car back from California. They are stopped because their rear license plate has been stolen. But in the process of putting the front plate on the back the officer finds marijuana in the trunk and arrests them. Peter and Mary Jackson suddenly find themselves in trouble.

And the indications that something is really wrong begin to multiply. Mary has already noticed a dead cat tacked to a speed limit sign. As they ride back to town in the police car, they pass an empty RV with a doll lying in the dirt beside it. And the policeman seems to be a bit crazy, from his robotic voice to his threat to kill them. Even the sign for the town of Desperation has been painted over with the words "dead dogs," and a dead German Shepherd hangs from it. The streets are empty except for such incongruous items as three bikes in the street with their wheels up in the air. The chapter ends as the policeman leads the husband and wife upstairs in the municipal building to the jail. They have to step over the body of a young girl, and at the end of the chapter the policeman kills Peter by shooting him in the stomach.

The shocking ending to this chapter establishes a pattern that King will continue throughout the first part of the book. He introduces each individual or group that is gathered by the strange policeman, ultimately identified as Collie Entragian, with key facts about their background. As the reader becomes more and more aware of the situation in Desperation, tension increases. We don't know why all of these people are locked up in the jail, but we do know that something is very wrong. We also suspect that early attempts to either understand or correct the situation will not be successful.

King maintains the suspense by interweaving the introductions of the new characters and their stories with attempts to overcome Collie and escape from the jail. The Carvers, the owners of the RV, are the next to be introduced. They are already locked up in the jail, and Kirsten, their youngest child, is the dead girl at the bottom of the stairs. Ralph and Ellen, father and mother, play important roles in the novel, but their son, David, has characteristics that make him central to the plot and theme. Their story is interrupted by the introduction of the other key character, John Edward Marinville, "Johnny," an aging author who is trying to find a way to get back to his former glory as the one-time winner of a National Book Award. He is gathering material for a new novel by riding a motorcycle across the country. He is not entirely alone. Steve Ames has been hired to follow him in a Ryder truck. Steve has also picked up a hitchhiker, Cynthia Smith. Tom Billingsley, a retired vet from Desperation, who can provide information about the town, the mine, and Collie, is the final occupant of the jail. Johnny's actual entrance to the jail ends the first part. He brings the news that Collie is disintegrating. This information raises more questions about what is happening in Desperation.

The second part further develops the questions posed by the opening. King presents a series of events that seem unconnected. Steve and Cynthia explore the Desperation Mining Corporation building, which they find has its lights on. They worry about the approaching sandstorm. At the same time David obeys a voice he hears and begins the actions that lead to his escape from the jail cell. Collie takes Ellen away. Finally David miraculously squeezes through the bars by covering his body with soap. All who watch are amazed when he manages to get his head through an opening that seems too small. This action is a further clue to the connection to divine intervention that this young boy possesses. The remainder of the second part unites most of the major characters, making the connections that relate the different events to each other.

The actions these characters take also provide further clues about what has happened and is happening in Desperation. Steve and Cynthia find part of a carved stone figure of a wolf in addition to dead bodies when they investigate the mining building. They both realize that just touching the figure arouses thoughts of strange sexual activities in their minds, a hint of the source of the evil they face. The others find mutilated dead bodies as they search for weapons in the municipal building. Collie takes Ellen to the mine outside of town, raising concerns about her safety for the reader. As another example of his powers, David manages to use Johnny's cell phone to contact Steve. The older man had been unable to make it work.

King moves to unite the diverse characters to advance the story to the next stage of the action. The novel progresses from an examination of individual activities to the more complex presentation of the working of a small community. The group from the jail decides to accept Tom's suggestion and meet Steve and Cynthia in the old movie theater, where they all can hide and decide what to do next. The group from the jail enters through the alley, an entrance long used by Tom and his drinking buddies. As Steve and Cynthia make their way to the theater they come across Audrey Wyler, a consulting geologist for Diablo Mining Company who has been hiding in the laundromat. By the end of the section all have assembled in the theater and begun to share further information, providing some answers to questions raised earlier in the novel. The reader learns that Ellen has been transformed into whatever was in Collie's worn-out body. She too returns to town determined to find the escapees. The reader anticipates her impact on the plans of the others.

At this point the reader still is likely to have only a vague idea of what may be going on. Steve realizes the stone wolf he found is connected ultimately to power. The object is also related to the mining company as is the Collie/Ellen transformation. David has learned from Tom that Collie has probably killed everyone in town. People had returned to town because of the reopening of the China Pit mine as a result of the new mining of copper. David also believes that Collie picked out the people he trapped on the highway. The reader, too, has wondered about a selection process. While King has still left more questions than answers, enough of a pattern is emerging for the reader to know one exists and to continue to believe that the answers will come.

In the third section, most of the characters bond together in the American West Theater, forming what Johnny thinks of as The Collie Entragian Survival Society. The name of the theater brings to mind the image of early settlers united against an attack. While Ellen's plans and inevitable attack provide the tension, King uses this part of the novel to bring together the information the characters need for the decisions that will lead to the final resolution of the conflicts. Just as he did when he brought the characters together, King moves from point of view to point of view so that the reader gains insight into the story from the perspectives of the key participants. The theater is a temporarily safe haven. Tom sets up an alarm system of beer bottles on the window ledge they used to enter. There is a portapotty for one of their basic needs, and they find a little bit of food. The building is locked, and no light emerges from it, but they know the person they think is still Collie will come looking for them. There are not a lot of places to hide.

As in all of King's novels the expected is never what happens. He moves back and forth between the survivors exchanging information and the thing that now inhabits Ellen's body. We gradually learn that she will not make the first attack directly. The thing in her body can control nonhuman life as well. Spiders spell out the word "theater" to reveal the location of those who have already escaped once. King maintains tension by intercutting the back stories the characters share with Ellen's future plans. Most of the stories reveal character, but two contribute to an understanding of the plot. Audrey provides background about the mining activities that have reopened the China Pit. The first method the company used to get at the copper was ecologically destructive.

The knowledgeable fiction reader knows that destruction of the environment often leads to the release of evil into the world. Audrey says that she was going to a meeting with the company's comptroller, Allen Symes, to discuss a change to a more ecologically friendly means of removing the copper. While the cougar Ellen has sent waits in the alley for her command to enter the building, Tom Billingsley, the old vet, explains the reasons for the mine being called China Pit. His story reinforces the clues the reader has already received about the mine's connection to evil. The first excavations produced some gold and silver. After the disaster the mine was abandoned until the recent strip mining for copper.

Tom tells them what happened while the Diablo Mining Company was digging for gold in the shaft called Rattlesnake Number One. Unfortunately the ground was not good for such a deep excavation. The company brought in Chinese laborers when others would not go down so far in such unsafe circumstances. They went down so far that they dug up a "waisin," an ancient spirit and went crazy from contact with it. A cave-in buried them. The reader realizes that this same spirit must be causing the current problems. Audrey tries to maintain a scientific position and denies the existence of the spirit. According to Tom's story, no effort was made to rescue the Chinese workers because they were not considered important enough. The opening of the mine was dynamited shut.

At the end of his story Tom decides to use the portapotty, but he really wants to get a drink that is hidden next to it. The cougar gets the command to attack. Suspense builds because Tom is also trying to remember something about Audrey that bothers him. Just as he remembers, the cougar attacks. King does not further tease the reader at this point. Before he dies, Tom does manage to reveal his memory to those who come to his aid: Audrey is taller than she used to be. She is tainted like Collie. While Mary remains with the dying man, the others run back because David is not with them. King introduces yet another crisis as Audrey attempts to kill the boy. The others manage to save him, but Ellen comes and takes away Mary. King continues the pattern of overlapping crises. This section of the book does not end with these events. David, who has passed out from the attack, is taken on a mystical journey that develops both the themes and the direction of the plot for the rest of the novel.

David possesses powers connected to his religious beliefs. Even though he is young he understands that these powers are not just magic and that, in trying to use them, he is not always able to accomplish what he would like. He discovered these powers when he successfully prayed for a dying friend's recovery. He now returns to the special place he and his friend shared back in Ohio, the place where he prayed. The two boys called it the Viet Cong Lookout. His guide on this supernatural journey helps him deal with the nature of God. David cannot understand how God could be so cruel as to let his mother and sister die. His guide, explains that there is a purpose to God's apparent cruelty and uses the analogy of God as the miner and humanity as the mine. David will still work through his relationship to God for the rest of the novel. The information his guide provides is in the form of a vision. They fly over the mine and the powder magazine containing ANFO, a combination of ammonium nitrate and fuel oil. King does not reveal all that David learns at this time, just enough to provide some answers and generate suspense about future events. The reader knows the mine must be destroyed; now the question is how the group will accomplish this task.

Part Four focuses on the culminating events at China Pit. King continues to shift back and forth among the characters. Mary, who is being held for the next body exchange, works to escape at the same time that the remnants of the group decide on their next action. Ellen, who is beginning to fall apart, returns to get Mary. When David awakens, he tells them much of what he has learned. His mother is dead, but she will not rest as long as Tak, the evil god or demon, inhabits her body. The biggest revelation is that Entragian, who is dead, did not bring them there; God brought them there to stop Tak. David also has a different version of the story of the mine than that told by Tom. The details about the miners and the depth of the mine change, but David is able to amplify the information about Tak: that is, the miners broke through into a chamber piled high with statues of some of the more predatory animals of the region, coyotes, snakes, wolves, and spiders. They uncovered a round hole, a well that is Tak's place, the source of the evil.

King provides this information at this time because it is necessary if they are to overcome the evil. It is also the central component in the conflict between David and Johnny. Johnny does not want to believe, but David knows he must convince this man if they are to succeed. David is also able to provide information about how the current emergence of Tak occurred. King now presents the answers to questions he has raised at the same time that he maintains the suspense by introducing new mysteries. We learn that Cory Ripton, who hates the mine safety regulators, decided to enter the mine and collect souvenirs before officials came onto the scene. He is Tak's first body, and he begins the destruction of the blast crew who made the discovery. Cory needs to find a new body and gets Brad Josephson, who has a great one. Tak is such a powerful force that the body it occupies is stressed. The disintegration begins at the site of any weakness or illness. Ironically Tak moves from body to body across breaths like a kiss.

While Johnny listens to this information he still resists an acceptance that would acknowledge God and divine desires. King makes a point of telling the reader that Johnny's wallet falls out of his pocket. We know that must have some importance, but we can only think in terms of money and credit cards should he leave the group and travel on. This incident is an example of the new questions King introduces to maintain suspense as he moves toward the final resolution of the story. When Johnny walks away David inspects his wallet and discovers a picture that validates the boy's vision in an amazing manner: a photograph of three men in front of a bar in Vietnam called Viet Cong Lookout. David met one of the men in his vision of the land of the dead.

King counters this revelation with the group's discovery of Mary's escape. The author then turns to Johnny, who finds the keys to an ATV and is ready to leave. He thinks back to the miracles he associates with David's actions. Activities in the various locations begin to occur at the same time. Ellen tries to keep track of Mary and the Ryder truck with most of the group as she sends a wolf to attack Johnny. The reader realizes that the balance of power has shifted in favor of good rather than evil. As the novel moves to the final confrontation, the questions become how will the evil be destroyed and who will be alive at the end.

David leaves the truck to return Johnny's wallet at the same time that Ellen chases Mary because her badly needed fresh body is escaping. Johnny confronts the wolf before David arrives. His only defense is to throw a hammer at the charging animal. He thinks his throw is off and prays that it is good. At that moment he feels that a power is helping him, and the hammer hits the wolf between the eyes. When David arrives Johnny still resists until the boy returns the wallet and talks about the photo. Johnny was his guide in his vision, because the vital man who was Johnny died while he was in Vietnam. David explains that a person who no longer changes or feels is dead. The scars David saw on his guide's wrist are the times Johnny tried to kill himself. This information both motivates Johnny's decision to stay and help and leads the reader to an acceptance of this character's later decision to sacrifice himself for the good of the group. Even though David tells Johnny that God can raise the dead this man feels it is too late. Johnny actually becomes two people as his interior forces fight to arrive at the decision to stay or go. Finally Johnny accepts the path toward God represented by David.

The spiritual conflict, with its connections to the thematic battle between good and evil that is at the center of this novel, becomes physical as Ellen chases Mary. When Mary escapes, Ellen is forced to enter the body of an eagle and hide in the mine waiting to attack David. After Johnny decides to work with the others he has a seizure that sets up another set of questions because he denies that it is what David calls a God bomb. The reader knows that Johnny is hiding information. The group organizes for the final confrontation with Tak. King maintains the tension because the reader knows not everyone will survive. Johnny takes charge. We know he hides the full extent of his plans from the others. He even acknowledges that God chose him because he is a good liar.

While David is certain that God wants him to die, Johnny's actions move him toward his own self-sacrifice and the protection of David through his telling Steve to grab David at the appropriate moment. When the eagle attacks, Ralph sacrifices himself for his son. David wants to go on but is prevented by Johnny, who takes something from the boy's pocket at the same time that he places something in it. He tells the boy he is excused early, a reference to a note at the Viet Cong Lookout. Johnny then tells all of the others to go back and continues on his own with the ANFO. With much trouble he goes down into the hole to the source of the evil. The shotgun shell he took from David's pocket just fits the opening and works as the primer when he hits it with a hammer, causing an explosion. He thinks of David as he dies.

The final section of the novel deals with the survivors. They pile into the truck cab and race away from the mine. They feel the explosion when China Pit falls in on itself. Once on Highway 50 they pass David's RV as they return to Mary's car. They decide on the story they will tell the police, a simple story. They believe the government will cover up these events just as it has done with Roswell, a town not too far from them known for UFO sightings. David reaches into his pocket and finds a piece of paper that answers the last question in the novel: what did Johnny leave him. The paper is the excuse that David had hung up in Viet Cong Lookout when he went to visit his friend in the hospital. It contains the words "excused early." Johnny has added a message of his own that includes a reference to the Bible stating that God is love. As David and Mary follow the others down the road he prays. King acknowledges that the most difficult action is to continue living at the same time that he gives the reader a method for doing just that.

The Regulators

The plot structure of this novel demonstrates some of the differences associated with the Richard Bachman persona that King adopted. While *Desperation* focuses on a religious conflict between good and evil, *The Regulators* frames that conflict in the context of popular culture. The novel is organized more simply than those associated with the King name. After the opening material, *The Regulators* is divided into a series of chapters headed by information about place, time, and date introduced by some kind of written artifact such as a postcard or article. The prefatory material immediately establishes the focus on popular culture with a reference to two of its masters, Jim Thompson the author, and

Sam Peckinpah the film director. The tone is set with a quotation by Steve McQueen from the western film *The Magnificent Seven*, "Mister, we deal in lead" (13). King indicates that this book will deal with life and death issues and suggests the influence of the thriller and the western film.

The relationship between the individual and the group is also altered. Tak remains localized in the body of a young boy, and the action is concentrated on a single block of a small Ohio town and the people who either live or visit there. Tak and the language it uses remain the same. Most of the characters from *Desperation* reappear, but they often function in different ways and in altered relationships to each other. Rather than a group of strangers who are thrown together, most of these people know each other. As a group they represent an archetypal image of an American town in the Midwest, a typical area of the country, the perfect site for an examination of the operation of the ideology associated with common people.

The postcard that introduces the first chapter is an ideal example of the novel's use of everyday objects that become representative of popular culture. The card was sent in 1994 from Nevada to Audrey Wyler in Wentworth, Ohio. Her brother tells Audrey of a breakthrough with his son Seth. He also tells her he will phone with more news later. King sets up questions for the reader with this information. These questions are amplified when the date that opens the chapter is two years later. This shift in time establishes a pattern that will operate throughout the book. He also moves from the postcard to shifting points of view of the inhabitants of Poplar Street in Wentworth on the afternoon of July 15, 1996, the site and date of the major action in the novel. Time shifts from chapter to chapter are initially indicated by citing the exact moment that each event occurs, but this scheme breaks down with the general disintegration that occurs toward the end.

King carefully sets the scene. An experienced King reader knows that something dreadful must happen when a novel opens with a description of a perfect summer day in a perfect town. The threat of thunderstorms later in the day is both real and metaphorical. King's introduction of this threat indicates a different use of information in this novel. The reader is often given hints about upcoming events before the characters. This advance warning creates another form of suspense, the anticipation of something known rather than the mystery of the unknown that dominates *Desperation*. In *The Regulators* the reader waits for events, but just as in life things never happen exactly as we think they will. While we may be ahead of the characters, King always surprises both them and us. Even without the hint of thunder we know that the peaceful scene on Poplar Street cannot last. If the reader has read *Desperation*, this novel feels like a déjà vu experience. Characters with familiar names appear slightly or greatly altered. In addition to questions about what will happen in this book the reuse of names raise concerns about connections between the two. The reader might even feel as if she or he has entered a parallel universe to that of *Desperation*, where everything is familiar and everything has changed.

The Carver children are the first to appear. This time Ellie Carver is the older child and her brother is Ralph. They add to the atmosphere of the scene when, like other siblings, they bicker on their way to the local store for a snack. From his lawn Brad Josephson watches Cary Ripton, a high school baseball player, deliver the Wentworth *Shopper*, a weekly paper. Johnny Marinville sits across the street playing his guitar. King uses the paperboy's route as a means of introducing the rest of the inhabitants of this block of Poplar Street. Each person provides a shifting perspective on the neighborhood. Gradually small elements disturb the summer idyll. Cary sees a van on the street. He thinks Mrs. Wyler, who lives in the only neglected house on the block, may be standing at the door with no clothes on above the waist. Cary thinks she is strange, as is her nephew who lives with her. Her husband died a year ago at the same time that the Hobarts, whose house is still empty, moved away.

King presents these events as clues, but the reader can only store the information away because it has no meaning without further clues. As Cary thinks about the dead man, a red van approaches the corner. A blue Acura also moves down the street while Cary talks with Mr. Jackson, a college teacher. Other inhabitants of the block play with a dog, and Cary shifts his attention to the friend of one of the teens, a red-haired cheerleader. King increases the tension by telling us that Cary will die a virgin and a backup shortstop since we have already learned that he will be first string next year. The red van moves as the introductions continue, including the presentation of the local retired vet, Tom Billingsley, and the ex-policeman, Collie Entragian. The van has a strange chrome item on its roof. A Ryder truck breaks down next to the store. No one notices it or the shotgun pointing out of the window of the van. As it begins to thunder King breaks the narrative with an artifact indicating a transition to the next chapter.

This time the artifact is a newspaper article about four people being killed in a drive-by shooting in San Jose. The people are identified as members of the Garin family from Toledo, Ohio. Only one child, Seth, survives uninjured. The reader now has another piece of information to connect with the first postcard. In addition, the drive-by vehicle is a red van. Here suspense is created by advance knowledge and anticipation. As the chapter opens, Steve Ames appears as the driver of the disabled Ryder truck. He also notices the strange red van and feels something is going to happen. The reader shares his feelings. At that instant the shotgun fires, and Cory and his newspapers fall. Gary and Cynthia, who works at the store, save the two children, Ellen and Ralph. Everyone on the block reacts. While some, at first, think it might be a backfire, Johnny's experience doing research in Vietnam during the Tet offensive leads him to believe it's a shot. There are two fatalities from the visit of the red van, a paperboy and a German Shepherd dog that distracted the shooter from the two Carver children. King uses the reactions to this incident to further introduce the inhabitants of the block.

The next artifact used to mark a new chapter proves to be a key to understanding the incident even though the reader cannot fully appreciate it at this point. The entry from a guide to movies on TV describes a film called *The Regulators*, a western about rampaging vigilantes. At first these characters seem to be supernatural, but they are actually the post-Civil War veterans who often frequent the genre, this time as the bad guys. As King returns to the story, vans of different colors appear at the various entries to the block of Poplar Street that is the focus of the story.

The reader now anticipates further violence. Their arrival establishes a pattern that will prevail for the remainder of the novel. The advent of the vans signals a new attack on the block. While they retire, the neighbors react and assess their situation. Each subsequent appearance of the vans brings an escalation of the violence. In the early chapters the violence also alternates with further information about the characters. Such knowledge can help the reader anticipate which of the characters might have the necessary traits to survive and help the others. The characters' understanding is behind that of the reader. But they also gradually begin to figure out what is happening to them. Attempts to phone for help prove useless. Later they find that they cannot even leave the block to get help. Both reader and characters realize some strange power has taken over this block and is the precipitating force in the ongoing attacks. King gradually presents the two people on the street who are most involved in both their own personal torments and those that destroy the block, Audrey Wyler and her autistic nephew, Seth. Their back story provides the connection to *Desperation* and the source of evil in *The Regulators*.

The introduction of the next artifact provides clues about the vans and the people in them. An article from a magazine deals with the licensing of Motokops action figures and accessories based on a Saturday morning cartoon series. These characters ride around in futuristic vans. There are both good and bad characters, including Colonel Henry, Snake Hunter, Bounty, Major Pike, and Cassandra. The vans have wheels that fold up and wings that extend from the sides. The various colors are associated with specific characters. The inhabitants of the vans that visit Poplar Street are combinations of these cartoon characters and those of the movie *The Regulators*.

After the visit of the vans and the death of more neighbors, King turns to Audrey and Seth. The reader learns that Seth and his family, at the boy's insistence, visited a mine outside of the town of Desperation, and an evil force known as "Tak" has gained control of the boy. The only time that Tak does not like to be in the boy's body is when Seth is on the toilet. Tak also controls Audrey and her late husband Herb, driving the man to suicide. Audrey survives because she has a strong memory from her youth, a weekend spent with her friend Janice Goodlin at a mountain resort in upstate New York, a hotel called Mohonk Mountain House. The best time during the trip was a Saturday picnic in a beautiful meadow with a gazebo-like structure where they could enjoy lunch and conversation. Audrey retreats to this place and time to gain relief from the domination of Tak. She must return to the present because she feels an obligation to care for Seth, who is not always under the control of Tak. This evil force maintains a parasitic relationship with Seth, its host, but is limited by his abilities. It must act and think like the boy even though its desires may be more adult. On this particular day Audrey realizes that Tak has become stronger and that something is going to happen. When she looks outside and sees the dead bodies she realizes that Tak has embarked on some plan.

The reader now has the majority of the clues necessary to understand what is happening on Poplar Street. The vans and the characters who drive them and shoot from them combine Seth's interest in the Motokops and western films, especially *The Regulators*. Tak uses the boy's images to bring destruction to the neighborhood. The characters do not yet have all of this information and can only react to the events.

Audrey begins to understand earlier than the others and has to formulate a plan to escape from Tak in a way that will allow her to warn the neighbors and save herself and Seth. At first the two groups work independently. The neighbors come together to try to survive the series of attacks from the vans while Audrey thinks back over the past as she tries to cope with the present. The reader has access to information from both groups and can put together the clues more quickly.

While the neighbors, led by Johnny, who assumes the leadership role, puzzle over the events, the reader begins to understand that some of the stranger aspects of the attacks have their source in Seth's mind. Bullet holes are not real but like a child's version of what a bullet might do. The strange animals that appear toward the end of the siege are manifestations of a child's drawings. The houses and the landscape of the Midwest become the western world of Seth's imagination as interpreted and created by Tak. More neighbors die trying to leave the confines of the block, but the rest of the community that surrounds this space has disappeared, replaced by an alternate universe of the TV and film westerns. Only when Audrey manages to escape because Tak is busy do the survivors understand fully what has happened. She plans to return to her house and save Seth by taking him off of the toilet. She has doctored his chocolate milk with a laxative. Just as she is about to rescue him with Johnny's help, Cammie Reed, who blames Audrey for the death of one of the twins, enters the house. Tak waits to return to his host body, but when he sees what is happening he enters Cammie and causes her to shoot Audrey and Seth. Tak kills Cammie when it tries to enter her. Only Seth could contain this force. It is lost without a host. Seth has already escaped from his body before he is shot. The same is true of his aunt. Once Cammie dies the world returns to the reality that existed before the appearance of the vans.

The novel ends with a letter from 1986 on stationery from the Mohonk Mountain House (a real hotel in New York State). Patricia, who is on her honeymoon, writes her friend Kathi about a strange event she has experienced. Kathi loves ghost stories, and her friend describes her encounter with local spirits. The two ghosts appear at a gazebo in a meadow that is now named after them: Mother and Son Meadow. Their first sightings occurred in 1982. Patricia describes the beauty and peace of this particular spot. The woman is in her thirties and the boy is six. They always wear the same clothes. Especially distinctive are the boy's cowboy boots. They seem to be more solid than ordinary ghosts. While Patricia never actually sees the ghosts, she does feel a presence in that meadow, and she finds strange artifacts that she sends her friend. The first is a woman in blue shorts, an action figure doll, but not one that anyone can recognize. The second item is a child's drawing. King includes this image at the end of the novel. The drawing depicts a woman with a child in cowboy boots standing next to a gazebo watching the sun behind the mountain. The reader knows from all of the evidence that somehow Audrey and Seth have transported themselves back to that perfect moment in Audrey's past, her place of refuge. The discarded doll is Seth's favorite Motokop, Cassie. They have escaped the present and Seth's autism to live forever in Audrey's perfect day.

CHARACTER DEVELOPMENT

As is often the case in King's work, characters are secondary to the story. While many of them are fully developed, when the novel is driven by action they are less important. *The Regulators* as the more action-oriented work is less dependent on them, and the characters in this novel, with the exception of Audrey, are less introspective. *Desperation* is concerned with larger issues relating to good and evil, and its characters are developed in greater depth because of the decisions they will have to make and the roles they play in the novel. Most of the characters appear in both novels. Some may play more important roles in one than in the other, and a few retain similar traits and relationships in both. Others are transformed from book to book. In some cases fathers and children change places, and in others people are good in one novel and evil in the other. Some secondary characters and one primary character only turn up in a single work. While Seth plays no role in *Desperation*, he does have his counterpart in David, an older child with a different kind of power. In general, the distinctions in the presentation of the characters in the two novels provide an interesting example of the similarities and differences between them.

David Carver

David is a recent manifestation of the troubled children or adolescents that King features in his works. The innocence of the young allows them to believe in the supernatural when adults would be too jaded by experience to trust what they see. For example, Bobby Garfield of *Hearts in Atlantis* can see the men in yellow coats, whom most adults ignore. David is different from other youths because he is driven by a serious religious conviction not often evident in King's works. He has come to his beliefs because of an experience with his best friend, Brian Ross. While the doctors find Brian's case hopeless, the intensity of David's prayer heals the boy. David's encounter is with God rather than the usual monsters of the supernatural in King's work. A voice tells him what to do, and he is able to get out of the prison cell in Desperation and begin the process of saving the others. David also experiences revelations through dreams when a guide takes him back to the tree house he shares with Brian. Its name connects his world with that of Johnny Marinville: Viet Cong Hideout is also the name of a bar Johnny frequented in Vietnam. The dream is one example of the journeys David makes during the course of the novel. Each is a form of a trial and a learning experience, from the family vacation that places their RV on Highway 50 to the entry of the mine and the source of the evil. David's larger journey is spiritual as he questions the nature of God and his plan for the world. At the end of the novel he is prevented from sacrificing himself by Johnny, who has had his own vision.

Seth Garin

Of all of the gifted children in King's works, Seth possesses the gift that is the most difficult for a child to deal with. His autism separates him from his family and the normal world of a child. While he enjoys certain aspects of the culture of childhood such as action figures, TV shows, and films, he cannot communicate easily with the world. He only talks freely when his parents approach Desperation on a trip to visit their college friends in California. Seth is drawn to the mine and becomes the host for the evil trapped in it. His parents' and siblings' deaths are the first attributed to Tak, the parasite that has invaded him. During the rest of the novel Seth attempts to protect some of his own identity against the ravages of Tak. His Aunt Audrey describes a rare moment on Halloween when he is able to communicate his desire to dress as a pirate. They go trick or treating, and he looks and acts normal. Tak was absent during this time. At the end he manages to hide his strength from Tak. Even though he dies he does free himself of the evil.

Johnny Marinville

Johnny Marinville is identified by his full name, John Edward Marinville, in *Desperation*. In both books he is the National Book Award–winning author of *Delight* and the former husband of Terry. But he has a darker and more complex personality in *Desperation*. In this book he is on a cross-country motorcycle trip to attempt to find a way to get back to his writing. In a sense he is also a variation on the stereotype of the reformed hard-drinking writer who has to now find a way to get back to his craft. His character gains depth when he has to decide to stay and help David, ultimately sacrificing himself in the fight against evil rather than escaping. In *The Regulators* Johnny has made peace with himself and his past. He has found a new life by moving to the quiet of this Midwestern town. He now writes children's books about a cat detective.

In both novels he has had some association with Vietnam and the violence represented by American involvement in that country. This experience and the observational skills he has developed as a novelist propel him into a leadership position in each work. He understands people and the reasons for their actions. The peace that he has found in *The Regulators* helps him survive. But the more interesting and troubled Johnny of *Desperation* demonstrates even greater strength through his sacrifice. The Johnny of *The Regulators* is a man of action. In the other novel he is often unable to move until the end, when his own encounter with God allows him to accept his role in saving David and the others.

Audrey Wyler

In *Desperation*, Audrey Wyler works for the Diablo Mining Company as a consulting geologist. While she seems to be a good person who is concerned about the environment Audrey has not avoided contamination by the evil force released from the mine. She is killed when she attacks David. Tom notices that she has been infected because she is taller than she should be. Prolonged time spent in the town contaminates her. She plays a much larger role in *The Regulators*. As the aunt of Seth she is most familiar with the actions of Tak and is the first to know what is happening on Poplar Street. Audrey has suffered greatly from her contact with Tak, even losing her husband to this evil force. She endures and ultimately triumphs because of her love for Seth. She will not abandon the boy to save herself. She gives the others the information they need to understand the events on the street and then finds a way to save herself and Seth. In both novels she is basically a good person trapped by circumstances. In *The Regulators* she is able to conquer the same force that destroys her in *Desperation*.

Collie Entragian

In both novels Collie is connected to the police. In *The Regulators*, he is an ex-cop and a character in the neighborhood. His neighbors think he was dismissed for graft, but he was really framed by a false drug test. He has now sunk into alcoholism because he is unable to get his life back on track. The attacks in the street help him become his old self because he can return to the heroic activities of his former job. He finally dies, killed by mistake by one of the Reed twins. He has already been taken over by evil in *Desperation*. Even though his body is disintegrating, he brings most of the characters together when he traps them on Highway 50 and takes them to the jail. He is also responsible for killing many people. He is not really a person anymore but rather the first example of the magnitude and scope of the evil emanating from the mine. Tom tells the others that Collie's name is short for collier because he came from a Wyoming mining town many years ago. He helped close the mine and then became one of Desperation's full-time deputies. The real Collie had a limp as the result of an accident, but his takeover by the evil has eliminated the limp, the first clue about how the possession changes an individual. Collie is a person who is caught by circumstances in both novels. He is not a bad man, but he is changed by events he cannot control.

THEMES

The thematic development of the two novels illustrates the difference between King writing as himself and as his alter ego, Richard Bachman. While some ideas are shared, *Desperation* focuses on concepts relating to the nature of good and evil in the lives of humans and their environment, and *The Regulators* is more concerned with the impact of elements of popular culture. Both present worlds infected by evil, and the source of evil in both cases is the mine in Nevada near the town of Desperation. The evil in this mine traces its origin back to early mining activities and the death of Chinese workers trapped because of bad mining practices. Both also deal with contained worlds where the characters are caught until the source of the evil is destroyed. Such containment raises questions about the relationship between free will and destiny. The characters can only act or make decisions within certain boundaries. Steve and Cynthia try to leave Desperation, but they find they cannot escape. They must join the others. The same is true on Poplar Street, where all contact with the outside world is impossible.

The thematic concept of boundaries is central to both novels. Not only do both deal with worlds that trap the characters, they also develop ideas of the limits of the body and of release and containment of evil. The aptly named Diablo Mining Company opened the pit to mine gold. The history of the mine follows the general trajectory of mining in the United States, exploitation of the workers, and increasing ecological degradation until the strip mining for copper of the present. The initial mining and the reopening of the pit also provided possible exits for the evil trapped there. The actions of people and their greed are responsible for making the release of this ancient force. But in both novels the evil needs further assistance to emerge and act in the world. While the source may be supernatural, the force needs a human host, thus raising questions about the origins of malevolence in society.

In both novels evil is associated with the word "Tak." Tak's influence is more pervasive in *Desperation*, and its range is wider. But still the characters work to contain it. In *The Regulators* Tak is confined to one body and has a limited range of influence in that body. It does seem to be able to work changes in the block, but its power is limited by space. In both novels Tak is more powerful than the human body it inhabits. In one book it moves from body to body because its force is so powerful that it attacks any weakness, accelerating the effect of any disease until the host body falls apart. An animal is an even poorer host and may only survive for hours once the parasite enters. Seth proves to be the only host who can contain Tak. His autism provides a shield against the outside world that allows Tak to survive in him. Tak's interaction with human hosts suggests aspects of the nature of evil.

In both works evil needs human contact to operate. The ultimate source of evil may lie outside of humanity, but people are necessary to activate it. Most people cannot deal with evil by themselves. In both novels people must come together to understand and combat this force. In *Desperation*, both the threat and the scope of the evil is larger. More people die, and there is danger of contamination extending beyond the boundaries of the town and the mine. The book also deals more directly with the nature of evil and human behavior. The characters are aware of the necessity for making choices and the implications of those decisions in the battle for control of the town. Tak can even employ the natural world, summoning animals and sandstorms to attack the humans. But the humans are constantly aware of the need to make choices for either good or evil. The presence of David is the visible manifestation of the need to take a stand. His religious beliefs and his contact with the spiritual world and the voice of God force the others to acknowledge the difference between good and evil. The acts he performs place the supernatural in the realm of the religious miracle. Tak's actions connect the novel with the horror genre, but David's activities move to the level of the more universal beliefs connected with organized faith.

In *The Regulators*, evil takes the shape of artifacts of popular culture, genre novels and films, and Saturday morning cartoons. The street eventually is transformed into a child's image of the West, but the fact that the images come from Seth limits the impact of the evil that is presented. Rather than making conscious choices, the characters in this novel are forced to react to events. Their responses are a result of their natures, but they are not drawn to do bad things. Only at the end of the book do the neighbors attack each other. And even then their actions are influenced either directly or indirectly by Tak. Only Audrey, who is isolated from her neighbors, acts independently. Ironically those closest to Tak and most familiar with it are those who know that they must choose to act rather than react in order to destroy this force. Seth has maintained some part of himself intact, and Audrey knows how to escape from Tak's control. Both of these characters operate out of a positive love for each other that survives their deaths and allows them a kind of eternal happiness.

The negative image of love is seen in the fractured relationships of many of the other neighbors. Those with the worst relationships are the first to go such as the couple Marielle and Gary, and Mary Jackson, who is returning home from an affair with another man. Belinda and Brad Josephson, who really care about each other, are alive at the end. Steve and Cynthia seem to form a relationship, and they endure. Johnny survives in this book because he is at peace with himself and his life. Cammie kills and dies out of a misguided sense of motherly love. Most of the families do not remain intact. King seems to suggest that modern life has within it the seeds of its own destruction. He finds fault with the very popular culture that he produces. But he does reaffirm the importance of love.

Love in all of its manifestations is questioned in *Desperation*. Again families are destroyed, but certain forms of love between people are important. Steve and Cynthia form a relationship that supports them. David holds onto his father as all that remains of his family. But he already knows the connection between faith and love when he saves Brian. Johnny's choice to enter the mine and destroy the evil comes both from a realization of what his life lacks and his experience of a contact with a higher power. He spends much of the novel thinking back over his failed relationships with women. He is drawn into martyrdom through his concern for David. Kindness is different from love. Mary reacts with kindness to pleas from Ellen, who has been taken over by Tak. She is captured and finally manages to escape and get rescued by the others. Tom Billingsley, who survives in *The Regulators* as the kindly retired vet surrounded by pictures of his clients, in *Desperation* is an old drunk who dies attacked by a cougar directed by Tak. Competence also seems necessary for survival. The real thematic strength of *Desperation* comes from a deeper consideration of love. Throughout the novel King confronts the conventional image of a God associated with love.

David and Johnny engage in lengthy discussions of God's lack of love or God's cruelty to his creations. David has difficulty accepting that the God he has embraced is the same God who allowed the deaths of his mother and his sister. God does not always respond to his prayers. Even though David feels he communicates through prayers, God at times remains aloof. Merit is not always rewarded. For much of the novel the characters puzzle over the possibility of any divine plan. They want to know why they have survived, why they were taken off of the highway, why they were brought together.

Finally David decides that God has chosen them to fight the evil of Tak. King's presentation of God in this novel is tied to a conversation about Gnosticism between Collie and Johnny that occurs during their first encounter. Gnosticism is a pre-Christian and early Christian sect considered heretical by other early Christians. Gnostics resolve the question of an imperfect world and a perfect God by ascribing creation to a lesser power. They are also concerned about the connections between the spiritual and material world. Collie challenges Johnny by telling him that he has never written a spiritual novel because he is not involved with his spiritual side. Collie uses the terms *pneuma* and *sarx*, which Johnny recognizes as Gnostic words for spirit and body. He translates Collie's statement to mean that he has ignored his spiritual life in favor of his body and agrees that the policeman might be correct (108–9).

When Johnny finally does recognize this spirit, he is able to destroy the evil by sealing it back up in the pit. He must lose his body and his life in the process. His final communication to David affirms his understanding that God may be cruel, but God is also love. In this note King unites the horror genre to broader concerns about the nature of good and evil. Johnny begins his message by telling David to stay ahead of the mummy (690), a reference to David's fear of a classic horror figure, but he ends with the biblical citation indicating God, is love. David finally understands that there are no limits to God, who can encompass everything expressed in the novel.

ALTERNATIVE READING: GENRE AND VARIATIONS ON A THEME

These two novels that appeared at the same time demonstrate many things about King's writing. They most clearly show the difference between King writing as himself and as his alter ego, Richard Bachman. Even though they share situations, settings, and characters they present two distinct approaches to the horror genre. Both explore the confrontation between good and evil as manifested in strange creatures and altered views of the real world common to the genre. But *Desperation* moves beyond genre considerations to a deeper examination of the basic nature of good and evil. *The Regulators* uses elements from other popular genres to create a terrifying universe.

At the most basic levels their structures and the way information is controlled lead to their different versions of the genre. As the section on plot development demonstrates, the reader knows less than the characters in *Desperation*. King manages the suspense in this novel by involving the reader in the analysis of the situation. In the beginning this structure is further complicated by movement between the various characters who have yet to be united in one place. King also inserts some back story of how people came to be on Highway 50. The reader learns of the connections between events and the reasons for events along with the characters. By employing this type of structure, King also involves the reader in a consideration of the complex themes of this work.

The reader is ahead of the characters in *The Regulators* and at the end has information denied to them. King moves back and forth between Audrey's world and that of the other neighbors at the same time that he inserts clues available only to the reader—such as the newspaper clipping, postcard, letters, and reports that precede new chapters. The reader begins to understand what is happening on Poplar Street before its inhabitants. In this case such knowledge reinforces the expectations of the genre. The reader anticipates the horror that is to come and waits to actually experience it. The sense of genre is fully developed through the references to other genres such as the western and the thriller novel. Rather than the deeper concerns of *Desperation* that push it beyond the traditional work of horror, this novel rejoices in being a part of the genre.

The reader recognizes the images of the western distorted by Seth's imagination and anticipates what is to come.

Violence is another element of the horror genre. While the level of violence is higher in *Desperation* because more people die, the images of destruction create a greater sense of violence in *The Regulators*. Much of the death in the mining town takes place before the novel begins. The disintegrating bodies inhabited by Tak are gruesome. But they are part of a greater evil that seems to be connected to the working out of major thematic concerns. The deaths on Poplar Street occur during the course of the novel and are more disturbing because of their association with the mind of a child and traditional genre images. They are not as thematically significant. There is a callous quality to the violence that emanates from the vans that cruise up and down the street. A paperboy and an innocent dog are the first to go. While such events are not unusual in the horror genre, King takes the reader into the mind of the boy just before he dies. A young girl dies at the beginning of *Desperation*, but the evidence of her doll left on the road beside the RV makes her loss more poignant. And the death of David's sister becomes an element in his examination of the nature of God.

The violence in *The Regulators* is tied to a more general presentation of elements of popular culture genres. King suggests that horror is not alone in its depiction of death and destruction. Saturday morning cartoons can generate a terrifying vision of the world of the future. Westerns look back to a past filled with confrontations between opposing forces ending in death and destruction. Novels in the thriller genre dealing with the darker aspects of crime and detection also lead to murder and betrayal. The novels associated with Richard Bachman have always seemed more extreme in their depiction of elements of the genre. In this one, the last by this alias, King questions the role of popular genres in generating forces destructive to society. In *Desperation*, popular culture is not the focus of the novel. Some of the references connect this book to other works by King. Cynthia worked in the woman's shelter of *Rose Madder*, and she likes the *Misery* novels. But the novel is more concerned with issues facing society such as ecology. King uses the horror genre in this novel to confront these broader societal problems. And its major connection to popular culture comes from its association with *The Regulators*. By presenting two novels as variations on a single set of circumstances and characters, King demonstrates the tremendous versatility of the horror genre.

4

The Green Mile
(1997)

Stephen King is always interested in innovation in his work. For *The Green Mile*, he experimented with the method of publication. Rather than releasing the entire novel at one time as is usual, he divided the book into six separate volumes that came out a month apart; the novel was later published as a single paperback. King gives the background for this experiment in the foreword to the first serial book. His foreign rights agent, Ralph Vicinanza, rented a house, and the realtor suggested that it looked as if it had come out of a Charles Dickens story. A later discussion with a British publisher focused on the way that Dickens used the serial form for the publication of many of his novels (ix). Eventually Vicinanza presented the idea to King, who recalled pleasant childhood experiences with *Saturday Evening Post* stories in his childhood (xi). King also liked the idea that he could control the reader by creating a suspenseful situation where the reader could not look ahead in the book to find out the resolution (xii). At the time that Vicinanza proposed the idea, King was already working on a short story about the electric chair, a subject that has fascinated him for years. King further liked Vicinanza's suggestion that he write the work in installments, mirroring the way the reader would see it (xiii).

King expands on the origins of the story in his introduction to the single-volume edition. He describes how he deals with his insomnia by telling himself stories when he can't sleep. When one story is told for too long, he has to find a new one. During one of these periods, his bedtime story was about a huge black man on death row, a first-person narrative told by a trusty who sold things off a cart. In this version of the story, the black man was supposed to make himself disappear before his execution. When King finally decided that the big man was a healer, rather than a magician, he realized that the idea was too good for bedtime (v–vi).

All of this information gives the reader insight into King's creative process. We can see the origins of a novel and the way he develops suggestions from others. He generously credits his wife for her input. When he discusses the writing of the novel, King also talks about the balance between reality and fantasy in this work. He had trouble recreating the 1930s world of the novel but felt that too much research might damage the mythic quality he wanted to produce (vii). He also demonstrates an ongoing interest in the structure of a work as well as its content.

PLOT DEVELOPMENT

In addition to the usual challenges confronting an author, the serial publication of *The Green Mile* generated new problems for King. The structure of the plot is even more important in a work that is issued serially, because the author has to solve the issue of reintroducing events from the previous volumes to a reader who may enter the work in the middle, as he explains in the "Author's Afterword" (464). King decides to follow Dickens's example and incorporate the information into the story. His wife's concern for the fate of Mr. Jingles, a mouse that lives in the prison, led him to what he calls a "front story," a term that can also be identified as a framing story. In *The Green Mile*, King balances the two storylines in each volume.

He begins the story in the present and varies the moment when his narrator moves back to the past. The movement between past and present adds complexity to the plot because the first-person narrator can reflect on the events and their causes both in the reliving and the retelling of them. The episodic structure causes these events to be retold from a variety of perspectives as the narrator reflects on what he has already written or suggests events to come. It is only at the end of the novel that the reader understands all of the reasons for the structure of the plot and the hints and omissions of details that have been part of its pattern. By introducing and then reintroducing information, King builds memories in his readers that mirror the memories of the narrator. Each volume was published under a separate title that suggested the central concern of the book. Most of the books have approximately the same number of pages, a necessity if each segment is published separately and priced the same.

Part One: Two Dead Girls

Even though the events in the novel are really driven by character rather than plot, King opens the first book with the recollection of a time, a place, and an object: the year 1932, the state penitentiary at Cold Mountain, and the electric chair known as Old Sparky or the Big Juicy. King slips in pieces of information about the warden and his wife, but the focus of the opening is the chair, which is behind much of the action. In what seems like a rambling story, elements of the execution and the room that houses the chair are introduced, as is the story of Beverly McCall, who avoided the chair and took the free name of Matuomi.

In E Block, the death row of the prison, the floor of the long corridor leading to the room with the chair is covered with green linoleum, hence the title *The Green Mile*. King indicates that the doorway leading to the room was so low that John Coffey, the huge black man of his bedtime story, had to "sit and scoot" to enter. The room could be so cold that during one execution several witnesses fainted. Even the careful reader would have trouble deciding which of these details are the most important. Names and dates of releases, executions, and deaths appear. At one point the narrator states that there was only one time when he questioned his job, which became the reason for writing the novel. But the overall structure of this chapter suggests the way that King will release information throughout the novel. Some details embellish the main points of a book or a chapter, but they also aid in creating suspense as the reader gradually picks up the most important information and remembers reading about it earlier.

The remaining eight chapters in this volume introduce most of the main characters in the novel. While each person—prisoner or guard—is briefly described, King concentrates on John Coffey's arrival on E Block and his crime. The narrator, Paul Edgecombe, is in charge of the block and learns more about Coffey's crime in the prison library. Because he was found holding their dead bodies, Coffey was found guilty of raping and killing nine-year-old twins who were abducted while they slept on their porch during warm weather. Paul is interested because the huge black man exhibits none of the violence that would usually be associated with such a crime. The other man on death row, Eduard Delacroix, is the next man scheduled to be executed. His life on the block is eased by the presence of a mouse he called Mr. Jingles.

While Paul awaits the final order for the execution, he suffers from a serious urinary infection. Three of the men who work with him are good, competent guards: Dean Stanton, Harry Terwilliger, and Brutus Howell (who is not brutal even though "Brutal" is his nickname). But the fourth guard, Percy Wetmore, is evil, stupid, and incompetent. He is able to keep his job because he is the only son of the brother of the governor's wife.

The volume ends with a foreshadowing of events to come. It is set at a point after the important incidents in the novel have taken place. Brutus discovers Mr. Jingles's former hiding place. In it are small splinters of colored wood and the smell of peppermint that were associated with Delacroix. This discovery leads Brutus to decide to ask for a transfer because he can no longer put men in the chair. Paul agrees. He also thinks of another prisoner, William Wharton, telling the guards that they would never forget him. The last sentence indicates that the two men did change jobs. Coffey was the last man they executed. This ending leaves the reader with many questions about the connections among all of these people and events. The story has not progressed enough for the cliffhanger endings King will use in future volumes, but the questions will impel the reader towards the next book.

Part Two: The Mouse on the Mile

The second book opens in the present and introduces Georgia Pines, the retirement/nursing home where Paul lives. This pattern will be repeated in all of the remaining books. By placing Paul in this setting, King is able to reintroduce elements from the previous book at the same time that he develops Paul's life at the home. Life in this setting is compared to that of Cold Mountain; both sites are involved in the eventual killing of people, either intentionally or unintentionally. Paul reintroduces Percy by comparing him with an attendant called Brad Dolan and then moves back to Mr. Jingles, the mouse of the title, and events on E Block. While Delacroix loved his pet mouse, Percy hated it from the beginning. In addition to introducing the nursing home, King reintroduces and further develops characters and events mentioned in the first book. He moves through various incidents in Paul's life to set up the major moments in the novel: Percy throws his baton at the mouse when it appears; a prisoner is executed; Percy does not understand how to act around men on death row; a white man's death sentence is commuted because of his class and race. All of these incidents both operate on their own right in the plot and set up situations in the future. Paul goes backward from the period in the first volume to tell what happened when Delacroix came into E Block and explains the animosity between this prisoner and Percy: the guard thinks that Delacroix tried to molest him when Delacroix fell against him accidentally.

In the middle of this volume, Paul admits that he never realized how far back he would have to go to relate Coffey's story. He understands that writing is a way for him to work through the feelings he has toward this man. Paul also indicates there may be more than one side to John Coffey, but he still wants the reader to believe that Coffey deserves his punishment. Paul establishes this attitude as a way of retracing his own experience with the prisoner and, at the same time, generating suspense in the novel. He then returns to the other prisoners.

Paul thinks that keeping the condemned men peaceful during their last days should be the main task of the guards. He accomplishes this by talking to them during quiet moments and encouraging a generally peaceful atmosphere. Percy never understands this aspect of his job and is unable to comprehend the fact that these men cannot be frightened because they have nothing to lose. His stupidity almost proves fatal for one of the guards when they bring in William Wharton, who would like to be known as Billy the Kid. His wrist chains are too long and he manages to get them around Dean's neck. Percy is too confused and frightened to react. This book concludes with the first of the major cliffhanger endings as Paul, who has drawn his gun, stares at Wharton, who dares him to shoot.

Part Three: Coffey's Hands

Rather than picking up where he left off in the previous volume, King increases the suspense by delaying the resolution of the crisis. This time Paul introduces Elaine Connelly, his special friend at the home and the ultimate audience for his writing. At this point in the story, she is used as a device to allow King to refresh the reader's memory about the preceding events. Elaine also encourages and assists Paul in his project. King finally returns to the point at which he ended the last volume. Brutus enters in the midst of the fight and hits Wharton on the head, ending the confrontation. King relates Percy's imagined molestation by Delacroix to an incident that occurs between Paul and Coffey.

Paul's urinary infection is very serious, and he is in a great deal of pain. Coffey asks to talk to him, saying he just wants to help. At first Paul is surprised and resists as Coffey puts his hand on Paul's crotch, but the jolt that passes through him stops Paul from pulling away. Suddenly the pain is totally gone. Coffey breaks eye contact, turns pale, and begins to gag. When his lips open, black insects fly out, turn white, and disappear. Paul does not understand what has happened, but he knows that he has experienced some kind of miracle. This incident so amazes him that he tries to discover more about Coffey and the murders. When he investigates further, he recognizes that the racism inherent in the legal system may be partly to blame for Coffey's conviction and begins to wonder if Coffey could be innocent.

Life continues both on and off the cellblock. Wharton acts up. The warden's wife, Melinda Moores, who has a brain tumor, comes home to die. Wharton grabs Percy when he forgets and comes too close to his cell; Percy is so afraid that he wets his pants, and Delacroix points it out to everyone. All of these incidents lead up to the bigger events in the novel. Once again, King ends the volume at a moment of crisis, as Percy steps on Mr. Jingles and breaks his back.

Part Four: The Bad Death of Eduard Delacroix

King again delays the resolution of the crisis that occurred at the end of the previous volume. Paul recounts his daily activities at the home, which include a visit to a shed on the grounds of the nursing home. More suspense is generated because he does not reveal the reason for his visit. Brad Dolan, Percy's alter ego, attacks Paul on his return. Brad's attitude brings Paul's mind back to Percy, and King sets up the situation again.

Back on E Block, Coffey asks for the mouse and repeats the miracle that he worked on Paul's infection. Everyone in the block is amazed as Coffey inhales the mouse's pain and injury. Mr. Jingles revives immediately, limps for a day, but eventually experiences a full recovery. Coffey once again reacts to the event by gagging and spitting out the black insects. This time there are witnesses to the incident, but everyone is more occupied with Delacroix's execution. King has given the reader many clues that build the suspense about the terrible thing that happens during the execution. Even the title suggests something bad without being specific.

King leads the reader to anticipate Percy's involvement in whatever is going to happen by including comments about how foolish the others were to trust him. The storm that occurs just as the execution begins lends atmosphere to the event. Percy has been promised a key job at the execution in exchange for his promise to transfer from the unit to a state mental hospital. The reader knows what to expect during the execution because another one was described in the first book. King foreshadows upcoming events when he has Paul acknowledge that he should have seen what Percy was doing. During the rehearsal, he did not understand the point of the questions Percy asked about the reason for soaking the sponge that is placed between the prisoner's head and the helmet connected to the electric chair. The sponge is soaked with brine to promote the conduction of the current. If the brine is not used, the transmission will not immediately kill, but will torture the condemned man. Paul sees that there is no water running down Delacroix's face and realizes Percy has deliberately omitted the brine as a means of tormenting the condemned man. But it is too late: the execution continues and the prisoner's head catches on fire before he finally dies. Even Percy had not anticipated the effects of his action. The guards threaten to put him in the cell with Wharton if he doesn't transfer. Amid all of this, Mr. Jingles runs away.

Since King has been building the suspense for the execution, he now has to produce another element to keep the story going. He ends this volume with a question. In reaction to what has happened, Paul begins to associate Coffey's powers with the warden's sick wife. Paul invites the guards, except Percy, over for lunch because he wants to discuss something away from the prison. They talk about Coffey's powers and the relationship between good and evil. Paul tells them about his cure and admits that he is positive Coffey is innocent. He has two reasons, the first having to do with his shoe. King leaves this clue unexplained until the next book.

Part Five: Night Journey

Paul reveals how hard it was to write about Delacroix's death. Dolan is again associated with Percy, and this connection brings Paul back to the day after the execution. He finally explains the allusion to the shoes: he gave Coffey his shoe and the prisoner could not tie the laces. This is important because Coffey is supposed to have given sausages from a lunch packet tied with string to the family dog before he took the twins. Paul realizes Coffey could never have retied the package and now understands that Coffey was trying to bring the young girls back to life when he was found holding them. Paul suggests that it was probably a white person who killed the twins. The terrible death of Delacroix leaves the men with the need to counteract this evil with something good. They agree to smuggle Coffey out of the prison to try to heal the warden's wife, Melinda. The suspense of whether or not they can accomplish this and the lack of details of their plot create a tension that replaces that of the death of Delacroix.

King carefully leads the reader through the stages of the plan. The guards know they must act immediately, before it is too late for Melinda and before they lose their nerve. They drug Wharton so he will not know what has happened and then lure Percy into a straitjacket and place him in the restraint room, supposedly as a reaction to what he did during the execution. While the trip and the cure work smoothly, King builds in new suspense elements. Coffey is very weak on his return, but his health is not the next problem. This volume ends with the guards' belief that they are safe but, as Paul suggests, there was more to come.

Part Six: Coffey on the Mile

In the final book, King's job is to keep the reader's interest as he resolves all of the questions raised earlier. Crises occur in both the framing story and the main one. King juggles the complex parallels between them as he moves towards the ultimate revelations. At Georgia Pines, Elaine saves Paul from Dolan because this time *she* is the one with important political connections. She begins to read what Paul has written while he works on the final chapter—as he says, "one last green mile" Once he takes the reader back to the prison, events occur quickly. Coffey, still ill, returns to his cell, and Percy is released. The guard once again forgets to confine himself to the middle of the green mile and moves too close to the cells. Coffey grabs him and exhales the illness he has taken from Melinda into Percy's mouth. Percy staggers away and, before the others can react, pulls his gun and shoots the still sleeping Wharton. Percy then becomes catatonic and never regains his sanity. Paul realizes that Coffey used Percy to kill Wharton. This gives Paul another idea, and he goes off just before Coffey's execution to do some investigating on his own. Once again King answers one question and poses another.

When Paul returns home he can only cry. He now knows too much, and his knowledge cannot change what is going to happen. He has solved the mystery. Wharton was the man who killed the two little girls. When the guards meet at his house again, they realize Coffey discovered that Wharton was the killer of the two little girls when he touched Wharton in the prison. Coffey has special skills, but he does not have the ability to analyze information. The guards know there is no way to prevent the execution of what Brutus calls a gift of God. Coffey says he wants to die: he is tired of being alone and cannot stand the pain he hears and feels. When he takes Paul's hands, the guard shares these sensations. While the execution goes smoothly, the men must deal with their own guilt over killing an innocent man. The connections between life and death are amplified by Paul's narrative. The fate of everyone involved in the story is detailed. Gradually the reader gets a sense of the tremendous passage of time and begins to wonder exactly when the "present" of the story takes place. King gives a few clues with references to television shows, but no real dates are revealed.

Paul returns to the present. The only death he has not described is that of his wife, Janice. He wants to show Elaine, who has now read most of the story, his current secret. They go to the shed where she discovers Mr. Jingles, who is much older but still enjoying life and chasing a spool. The mouse turns out to be at least sixty-four years old and Paul is 104. Brad enters, happy to finally discover Paul's secret. During their confrontation Mr. Jingles finally dies. Paul and Elaine bury the mouse, which somehow found his way to the home and Paul. Both man and mouse have shared the effects of contact with Coffey: even though they aged, they remained free from all illness.

King does not end the novel with the mouse's death. Instead, he turns to the last defining moment in Paul's life—the death of his wife in a bus accident on their way to a grandchild's college graduation. Jan dies in his arms. Paul calls for help and thinks he sees the image of Coffey, but the dead man cannot revive Jan. Her death leads Paul to question the difference between salvation and damnation. Now all he can do is wait for his own death. For him the green mile is very long.

CHARACTER DEVELOPMENT

Often in King's more traditional works the characters must react to a challenge presented by an evil force. From the vampire of *'Salem's Lot* to the satanic visitor in *Needful Things*, dark figures disrupt the lives of ordinary people. There are times in his fiction when the source of conflict comes from within a person, as with Carrie's special gift or the misguided desires that operate in *Misery*. *The Green Mile* belongs to this category. Usually in fiction that is constructed to keep the reader in suspense, elements of the plot impel the action forward. In this book the action is character driven. Even though much of the action takes place in the confined area of E Block, King traces the lives of many characters that contribute to the action. There are a few who are more fully developed than the rest, and they represent both the extremes of good and evil in humanity.

John Coffey

John Coffey embodies the mystery at the center of the novel. Paul's detective work and his subsequent solving of the crime reveal Coffey's innocence. While this mystery can be solved, the source of Coffey's powers is never defined. Paul cannot find out much about his past except for a few possible encounters others have had with him. He is a loner and a drifter, imprisoned in a large body and a small mind long before he reaches Cold Mountain. Coffey instinctively senses the difference between good people and bad people, and he knows how to make his power work. But his understanding of the world remains on the level of sensation, and the feelings he experiences cause him pain; he sees and feels more than he can stand. The guards may hate the thought of executing him, but he welcomes the release from pain.

While Coffey dominates the action, he remains an enigma, a symbol of a good beyond understanding. He may be seen as a gift from God, but no one can figure out what connection his existence and death have to the relationship between good and evil in the novel. Even his power is mysterious. He has connections to other traditional faith healers, and his initials connect him to Christianity. King makes references to his suffering and that of Jesus, but ultimately he is not a religious figure. Whatever salvation he brings is limited to relief from illness. He uses Percy to destroy Wharton, who embodies evil, but his understanding of evil in this man derives solely from Wharton's killing of the two little girls. Coffey represents action and reaction without real comprehension of the implications of those acts.

Paul Edgecombe

Paul Edgecombe is the other focus of *The Green Mile*. As he is the narrator, his perspective dominates the novel. More is known about him and his life than that of any other character. He initiates much of the action or reacts to events as they happen. In addition his comments and observations give the novel its meaning beyond plot and character. His long life and his experiences give the book its vision. He also provides the connections among all of the characters: as the first-person narrator, he must know all of them. But he has some limitations in his ability to deal with them.

Paul is the boss in E Block, but during the Depression no job is ever secure. He must be careful how he handles Percy who, because of his political connections, can get him fired. Some of the decisions Paul makes are motivated either by having to deal with Percy or by protecting the other men's jobs. In a sense, he is too good to understand the evil represented by Percy and Brad. He can deal with the ordinary criminal like Eduard Delacroix and the others he has seen on death row, but he is often unaware of Percy and Brad's schemes because he connects evil with stupidity and incompetence. Paul does his job well and is able to succeed in such projects as saving Melinda, because he can comprehend the ways in which goodness motivates people's lives. But the evil of Brad and Percy is beyond him. His limited understanding of good and evil may be the cause of his ultimate lack of faith and his inability at the end of the novel to distinguish between salvation and damnation. When so much of what happens in his life results from the actions of other people, he can see no divine pattern in the universe.

Percy Wetmore and Brad Dolan

As King so often indicates in the novel, these two characters are versions of the same person who appear at different points in Paul's life. They represent the banality of evil, one of the true horrors in the book. They are frightening because they are stupid, lazy, and incompetent, but they still have power over other people's lives. Percy never understands the role of a guard on E Block; he wants to antagonize rather than soothe the inmates. When he makes a decision, he is the cause of pain and suffering—as in the death of Delacroix and the injury to Mr. Jingles.

Percy is both racist and homophobic. But in the end his own stupidity and lack of attention to his job defeat him.

Brad is not as central to the action. He causes trouble for Paul, but in the end does not really affect the action. But he too poses a kind of terror for the reader: no one wants to think of this kind of person having a position of authority in a retirement/nursing home. He represents a fear about aging that many must face. His attitude towards the elderly is one aspect of prejudice. Both men show how the supernatural may not be as frightening as the evil that exists in ordinary people.

THEME

The themes in *The Green Mile* are a combination of such traditional concerns as the nature of good and evil and the relationship between past and present and more contemporary elements that are the result of Paul's perspective on the events of his life. Because he has lived so long, Paul can deal with issues in the 1930s, while also raising questions about racism, homophobia, and the validity of the death penalty. As the narrator of the text, he considers the role of writing and the impact of that act on one's life—an ongoing enigma for King.

The relationship between good and evil is reflected in the characters in the novel. Paul's longevity allows him to see what happens to good and bad people. His experience on E Block gives him insight into the arbitrary nature of human justice. He believes that Delacroix, who raped and killed a young girl and then killed six more people when he set fire to a building to hide the body, deserved to die, but Paul certainly does not see the way Delacroix suffered as justified. Paul believes that murderers go to hell, but he knows that some are executed while others have their sentences commuted. Arlen Bitterbuck, the Cherokee, killed a man while they both were drunk. His is the first execution described in detail. The man they called the President pushed his father, who was almost senile, out of a window, but since he was an important white businessman, his sentence is commuted. There is still some justice, as another prisoner kills him twelve years later.

What finally shakes Paul's faith is the death of Coffey, whom he knows is innocent; that event and the accidental death of Janice make him question the operation of both human and divine justice. King poses a problem that many have debated: why bad things happen to good people. While there is a certain justice in Percy's having to live the rest of his life under the control of people who might be just as evil and incompetent as he and ending up in the same institution that he was going to transfer to, this outcome is not an answer to the suffering of the good.

Paul's vision of the relationship between past and present is connected to his understanding of justice. He knows not only how people live but also how they die and can see whether or not their deaths reflect the way they lived. He can also see how the world has changed. Some attitudes may have changed for the better, but evil people still exist. Paul's life highlights the problems of the elderly and continues King's concern with aging, which was so well examined in *Insomnia*. Paul understands the physical and mental limitations of his advanced age, but he also values the perspective of memory that allows him to write his story. The events of the past are closer to him than those of the present.

The themes that relate more closely to the present seem to come more from King the author than Paul the narrator. Percy's homophobia generates the series of events that lead to his catatonic state. If he had not misinterpreted Delacroix's stumbling against him as the prisoner entered the cellblock, he would not have reacted as he did during the execution. His homophobia also leads him to adopt a super-masculine pose that contributes to his inability to deal with his duties as a guard on death row.

Both King and Paul underscore the effects of racism in the justice system. While Paul transfers from E Block after Coffey's execution, he cannot really question the validity of the executions of the real murderers that he participated in throughout his career as a guard. King stands outside of Paul when he pushes the reader to go beyond the narrator and look closely at the death sentence. Paul must remain a product of his time and the attitudes he absorbed. He changes as much as he can for a man who was an adult during the Depression. But King suggests that a flawed system is never just.

The most unredeemable character in the novel, William Wharton, does not live to be executed, but an innocent man goes to the chair. And there is no real justice operating in those who face death as opposed to those whose sentences are commuted. All of these examples of the failure of the system are combined with graphic descriptions of the process of electrocution. Even if methods may be different today, the effect on the individual and the sense of the moments leading up to it remain the same.

For King, then, the act of writing becomes a way to question problems facing contemporary society. But the importance of this act goes beyond that of protest against injustice. For Paul, the book brings the past to life and allows him to reflect on it. He is amazed at the doors that he unlocks by writing and how far back he must go to find the whole story. He even keeps a diary at Georgia Pines as a means of keeping track of the passage of time there. While King wants to create a certain mythic quality in *The Green Mile*, Paul's actions in writing his narrative give the book a sense of reality. He underscores the difference between a fictional world and the one that he presents. At one point he recounts that, unlike those in films, the phone in the room where the executions took place never rang. As he says, "In the movies salvation is cheap. So is innocence. You pay a quarter, and a quarter's worth is what you get. Real life costs more, and most of the answers are different" (88). He sees his work as reproducing the reality of the events he experienced.

At the same time there is a dangerous magic in writing. Both Paul and King have to come to terms with the good as well as the bad that must be described, as in the presentation of the death of Delacroix. A writer cannot avoid dealing with such a terrible event. If King is to remain faithful to his subject, he cannot avoid giving the truest picture possible of the awful as well as the beautiful. Honest writing demands much of the author. The effort Paul puts into his memoir mirrors the effort of King. Even though he is known as a prolific writer, King often reflects on the difficulty of doing his job well and the effort that task takes.

ALTERNATIVE READING: THE SERIAL FORM

As King acknowledges in his introductory material to this work, special techniques are necessary for the serial form. The use of this form raises questions about narrative structure and the traditional novel's organization it challenges. When *The Green Mile* originally appeared, people purchased a new volume every month for six months. Each book had to be somewhat self-contained in order to provide a satisfactory experience for the reader. However, if each book was too incomplete, King ran the risk of alienating his audience. At the same time, he had to provide enough suspense for people to come back for the next volume and even spend time anticipating it. Because a certain amount of time would pass between the publication of each book and the next, he could not rely on the reader's memory of the preceding events. He had to find ways to incorporate information about the previous volumes into the new one. Some of the techniques King used have been suggested in the section on "Plot Development." A further analysis of these techniques reveals the way in which *The Green Mile* differs from a more traditionally structured work.

King uses two devices to sustain the suspense from one book to the next. First, he incorporates clues about upcoming events into the text. Paul often uses the excuse of the effects of age on his memory to move back and forth in time. This tactic gives the reader hints about what is to come. These clues about the future both create suspense and move the reader along in the text. In a sense, they operate the way different stories do in soap operas. In this serial form there are what are called front burner and back burner plots. When a plot in the foreground nears resolution, the one in the background can come forward without having the story lose momentum. In *The Green Mile*, Melinda's illness is a back-burner plot until Delacroix's execution, when it moves to the fore. In this way King can create a series of climaxes that both keep the reader involved and provide some of the satisfaction of closure within the individual volumes. One story may have a resolution, but another takes over to create new suspense.

Within this organizational plan, King also incorporated the cliffhanger endings associated with the Charles Dickens model. Each ending is also slightly different from the others. The first ends by raising a question. Paul states that the Coffey execution was their last. For a long time, the reader believes that Coffey is guilty. The source of the reasons behind Paul's statement remains hidden until near the end of the novel. The end of the second book occurs at the moment that Wharton arrives and is choking Dean. Paul has his gun pointed at the criminal. The reader knows that Wharton does not die at this point because of the information Paul has already divulged but will not know how this situation is resolved until the next book. The third volume closes with Mr. Jingles's bleeding body. The thoughtful reader may anticipate Coffey's actions because Paul has already revealed evidence of his powers but must wait for the next book to confirm this solution to the crisis.

The next book ends with Paul setting the puzzle of his shoe and why he gives it to Coffey. After the horror of Delacroix's execution, this question returns the series to a less emotional and more intellectual level, which allows the reader to recover from the stress of the execution. The close of the fifth volume creates open-ended suspense: just when Paul and the reader think order has been restored and the guards have been successful in curing Melinda without causing trouble, Paul suggests that their problems were far from over. He sets the stage for his final confrontation with Percy.

The novel ends with Paul's life after the events in 1932, which is a kind of epilogue that answers any remaining questions about the fates of the participants. Throughout *The Green Mile*, King carefully employs various techniques to create suspense and yet provide a unified text for the reader. His revival of the serial form works on the level of narrative structure to create a novel that can be enjoyed as a series of texts or as a unified work. At the same time the nostalgia generated by this form suits the subject and setting of this book.

5

Dark Tower IV:
Wizard and Glass
(1997)

Wizard and Glass is the fourth novel in King's Dark Tower series, which includes *The Gunslinger* (1984), *The Drawing of the Three* (1987), and *The Waste Lands* (1991). As he explicates in the Argument, the opening section of the most recent addition to the story of Roland of Gilead, the entire series, including future novels, is inspired by Robert Browning's poem *Childe Roland to the Dark Tower Came* (xi). King continues by explaining Roland's origins and recounting the events in each of the volumes that precedes *Wizard and Glass*. The series presents a large set of characters, covers huge spans of time, and travels among a variety of worlds. King also blends many different genres in his development of the story of Roland and the people who are drawn into his world and his quest. In this addition to the series King includes elements from his other fiction. As he states in the Afterword, "I am coming to understand that Roland's world (or worlds) actually *contains* all the others of my making" (671). While King increasingly seems to be moving toward a fictional universe that unites his locations and characters, this tendency is most intensely expressed in the Dark Tower series and especially in *Wizard and Glass*.

The creation of such an elaborate vision gives King's fans the opportunity to make connections with other works they have experienced by this author. The reader becomes part of a group of insiders who share an awareness of associations with past pleasures. This kind of relationship to the works of an author or the films of a director is an important aspect of the popular culture experience at the end of the twentieth century; the reader or viewer may be a devoted fan who is extremely familiar with the work of an author or film director and awaits each new work, eager to find the relationships with another aspect of the artist's world. The experienced King reader turns to *Wizard and Glass* anticipating a reunion with the central characters of the series. There is added pleasure in being among those insiders capable of discovering the connections to other King worlds. In this novel King uses this familiarity with his works to create a story within a story. He begins the novel with the resolution of the cliffhanger ending of *The Waste Lands* and then moves to a story from Roland's past. The framing story resolves the suspense created at the end of previous volume in the series at the same time that its characters move into a sphere connected to *The Stand*. *Wizard and Glass* moves the reader through its various worlds and time frames as King examines the impact of these transitions and the meanings behind them.

PLOT DEVELOPMENT

King does not rely on the reader's memory of the events in the preceding novels when he begins *Wizard and Glass*. He recounts the important episodes in each of the books in the Argument. As many of the characters and their stories from the previous volumes in the series will reappear, it is meaningful that the reader recognizes them. The past is especially important to this novel since the main body is an extended flashback to Roland's youth. In addition to the evil characters who reappear from *The Waste Lands*, villains from *The Gunslinger* also return. The opening, Argument, provides a summary for the reader because the range of characters and events is so great that the details may be elusive for some, especially those who read the books as they appeared. Once King reestablishes the current situation of the central characters—Roland, Eddie, Susannah, Jake, and Oy, a billy-bumbler (a badger/raccoon/dog combination)—he takes up where the narrative left off. Jake has been rescued by Roland and Oy from the Tick-Tock Man, who is left for dead but in turn is helped by the even more evil Richard Fannin. Roland, Jake, and Oy join Eddie and Susannah and just make it aboard the insane train called Blaine before the decaying computers beneath the city of Lud totally fail, and Blaine releases the nerve gas that will complete the destruction of the city. They are able to board the train because Susannah, with the help of one of her alter egos, Detta Walker, solves Blaine's riddles, but the train holds them hostage. They strike a bargain: Blaine will release them if they find a riddle he cannot answer.

In addition to the Argument and the Prologue, the book is divided into four parts and an Interlude between parts two and three that separates the book into two halves. Each of the parts and the Interlude have titles—"Part One: Riddles," "Part Two: Susan," "Interlude: Kansas, Somewhere, Somewhen," "Part Three: Come, Reap," and "Part Four: All God's Chillum Got Shoes." These sections are divided into numbered chapters that also have titles. The titles of the main segments refer to events, and some chapter names reflect the passage of time by using lunar designations such as the "kissing moon" or the "demon moon." The chapters are further divided into small numbered segments that mark shifts in time and place as a means of organizing the parallel lives of the many characters. The organization of *Wizard and Glass* reflects its complexity as it moves through several different worlds and eras.

Before King moves to the Prologue that reestablishes the riddle contest, he provides a series of quotations that reflect the three main elements of the plot of *Wizard and Glass*. A selection from William Shakespeare's *Romeo and Juliet* suggests the love interest that is a major part of the flashback story. A scene in the Throne Room from L. Frank Baum's *The Wizard of Oz* sets up the central constituents of the framing story and connects this story to the flashback with the idea of the wizard and the witch so central to Oz. The third quotation, from *Childe Roland*, presents ideas of a happier past and their effect on the soldier's present, uniting flashback and framing story to the ongoing quest to reach the Dark Tower. The Prologue and the first section of the novel then establish the major elements of the framing story and indicate the flashback, providing immediate evidence of the importance of the concepts introduced by the quotations. Both of these sections have titles that suggest a variety of meanings. The Prologue is not just a simple opening of the novel but also an introduction to the future actions and relationships of the characters. Roland challenges Blaine in the riddle contest, and this challenge recalls Roland's role as a gunslinger, the initial challenge when he received that title, and the future events in the novel where he must face new trials. "Part One: Riddles" refers not only to the riddles necessary to defeat Blaine but also to the series of questions Roland and his group must face. In this section Roland attempts to defeat Blaine with riddles from past contests in Gilead. But Eddie is the one who actually conquers the train, by using knowledge he gained from his brother and nonsense riddles from his youth. No one character or one time period is enough to deal with the problems that confront those searching for the Dark

Tower. As the rest of the novel will further demonstrate, a plot this complex requires many kinds of heroic actions and many different kinds of solutions to those problems.

Once Eddie's riddles destroy Blaine, the group leaves the train to find themselves in a world different from the one they left in Lud. It is not the world that any of them have come from, but the King fan will recognize it as similar to the world of *The Stand*. Most of the inhabitants have died from a mysterious plague, and several of the characters from that novel exist in this world. But this world contains anomalies that set it apart from known places in King novels and contemporary United States. In addition to the usual brand names, there are also cars called Takers, a major league baseball team called the Kansas City Monarchs, and the fast food chain, Boong Boong Burgers. The thinny, a creeping destructive swamplike force that emits disturbing sounds, appears as they head down the turnpike trying to find their way back to the beam. Roland has encountered another thinny in the episode from his past that he will soon share with them. They have arrived in Kansas, a place with connections to another group—Dorothy and her friends, an association that will be amplified at the end of the novel. In this strange place where other worlds intrude so easily, Roland finally confronts a central event in his youth. Over a campfire he tells Eddie, Susannah, Jake, and Oy the story of his love for Susan and the other adventures of his stay in the town of Hambry in the Mejis region of Mid-World in a post-apocalyptic time.

The flashback, which comprises the major portion of *Wizard and Glass*, deals with three stories that gradually are united into a series of final confrontations. The first is that of the beautiful Susan Delgado, who has been sold to Mayor Thorin as a kind of concubine. The period leading up to the consummation of this relationship is complicated by her meeting with Roland, who is going by the name of Will Dearborn, and their love affair. Roland's arrival in Hambry is the second story. He and his two friends, Alain (Richard Stockworth) and Cuthbert (Arthur Heath), have been sent to this area as a means of keeping them away from the serious problems facing the Affiliation in Gilead. They are to assume new names and pretend to be sons who are being punished. Their supposed task is to count everything in the area for the Affiliation. The third story deals with the attack on the Affiliation by John Farson, also known as the Good Man, that is being mounted in the Mejis. Three men, known as the Big Coffin Hunters because of the blue coffin tattoos on their hands, are already in the area assembling war materials. One of them, Eldred Jonas, is a failed gunfighter who has been sent out of Gilead. He and his two helpers, Roy Depape and Clay Reynolds, are filling tankers with crude oil and assembling horses and oxen for Farson's coming attack on the Affiliation.

The three stories also embody three genres that merge into a single interconnected narrative going forward and backward in time. Susan and Roland are "star-crossed lovers," and their romance is mirrored in Roland's discovery of his mother's infidelity and in Eddie and Susannah's more successful relationship. The journey of the three boys is an aspect of the Arthurian legend dealing with the trials of knights, and it is connected to the quest of the mature Roland and his friends in the framing story. The final narrative contains elements of the war and western genres, including a range war and preparations for an armored tank attack. These aspects of the narrative are also reflected in the battles in *The Stand* and those aspects of the two genres in the framing story. But even though all these elements can be distinguished, in the novel they soon become entangled. King opens with Susan, but she leads to all of the other threads of the narrative. The actions of the central characters are set against the moons that mark the changing seasons of this rural community.

In the love story, Susan must balance her obligations to her Aunt Cordelia, who has arranged for the relationship with the mayor and who will also profit from it, with her love for Roland. He, in turn, must deal with his commitments to his family and friends and his passion for his first love. As the story progresses, love and duty become inseparable for both. Susan, because of her connection with the mayor and the community, has knowledge that is essential for Roland. He and his companions discover the plot to assist Farson as they go about their task of counting everything in the Barony. Those who are aligned against them operate in all three strands of the narrative and also connect them. Rhea, the witch who attests to Susan's virginity for the mayor at the beginning of the flashback, also works with the Coffin Hunters.

The three men entrust Rhea with the Wizard's Glass that allows her to look into people's lives. When Susan goes to her hut for the virginity test she sees Rhea looking into the globe and later gives this information to Roland. While the love story assists Roland and his friends with their tasks, it also generates an opposition that is ultimately destructive to the relationship. Susan and Roland suffer from the envy and hatred of Rhea and Cordelia, who form an alliance leading to the destruction of the young woman and a horrible act by Roland. Rhea and Cordelia join together and manage to convince the townspeople to burn Susan as the culmination of their harvest celebration. Rhea later takes over Roland so that he thinks he is killing the witch; but he actually shoots his mother, an event that Eddie, Susannah, and Jake watch through the Wizard's Glass.

A similar sequence of positive and negative forces is engaged when the young men pursue their jobs. The courtly attitudes they bring to this part of the world place them in conflict with the Coffin Hunters. The personal antagonism between the two groups also intensifies the public confrontation between the Affiliation and Farson's army. While the young men are actually able to defeat Farson this time, they only manage to delay his ultimate triumph. They trick his forces into self-destruction in the thinny. Roland thinks Susan is safe and once again chooses the quest over love (as he has done with Jake). Roland becomes so absorbed by the Wizard's Glass that he cannot function, and Alain and Cuthbert return him to Gilead on a travois of pine branches. The final scene of the flashback, the confrontation with his mother, does not occur in this part of the novel.

Roland, Eddie, Susannah, Jake, and Oy have listened to this story while spending the night on the turnpike looking down the road toward a glass palace. Roland tells them about his return to Gilead, and they resume their journey toward the palace when they find red shoes for all of them in the middle of the road. At the end of the novel, the *Wizard of Oz* story dominates the action. Since Roland has never heard it, they recount it for him. Of course there is an obvious connection between these travelers and Dorothy and her friends, even to Oy as a stand-in for Toto. They discover that they must put on the shoes to enter the Green Palace, but just as with the rest of the novel, nothing in this world is exactly normal according to their expectations. The Palace is beautiful, but it is also evil. The flags on the towers fly the mark of the Crimson King (a reference to *Insomnia*), a fact Jake knows without understanding how or why; he does not know it is also the sign of the Good Man.

For those of the characters familiar with *The Wizard of Oz*, the interior of the castle is a combination of that story and their experience with Blaine, an observation that brings the novel full circle, uniting its elements. When Oy imitates Toto and pulls back the curtain, the wizard is transformed into the Tick-Tock Man, whom they finally manage to kill. The man behind Tick-Tock who assumes the throne is none other than Marten Broadcloak, Roland's old enemy and the source of many of his family's problems. Marten, the sorcerer, now calls himself Flagg, the immoral shape changer behind *The Stand*. In yet another confrontation with this elusive evil force, Flagg manages to escape, leaving behind the glass ball. After the death of Roland's mother is revealed in the glass, all of the events of the flashback are completed, and the travelers continue once more to pursue the Dark Tower along the Path of the Beam. The major stories in this novel have been resolved, but the quest continues; the final confrontation between good and evil is yet to come.

CHARACTER DEVELOPMENT

As in the other works in this series, the complex plot of *Wizard and Glass* leaves little room for extended character development; only a few are multidimensional, with lives that extend beyond the exigencies of the story. Other than the information about Roland's youth, little new is revealed about the continuing characters in this novel in the series, and they seldom demonstrate moral ambiguity. The groupings of the good characters in both the framing story and the flashback reflect the series' ongoing use of the concept of the *ka-tet*, one from many, people united in their goals, found in the other Dark Tower novels. With few exceptions the characters in the flashback are presented as either good or evil in roles associated with their genres. Susan, as the love interest, is more fully drawn, as is the evil failed gunslinger, Eldred Jonas.

Roland

In a kind of prequel, King introduces the young Roland in *Wizard and Glass*. In addition to the seasoned gunslinger of the framing story, the flashback examines the young man and the events that shaped his attitude toward the world. The older man both physically and mentally reflects the harsh trials he has survived. The young Roland is just fourteen, but he has already survived the test of becoming a gunslinger. This trip with his two friends, Alain and Cuthbert, is his first experience outside of his home in Gilead, where he has left his father and mother. His father, Steven Deschain, is the twenty-ninth descendant of Arthur of Eld, a noble line. While Roland already demonstrates the leadership and planning skills that have enabled him to survive, he is naïve about some of life's experiences. His first encounter with love teaches him much about this word and at the same time reveals the deeper romance hidden in his practical exterior (248). His both finding and losing love so quickly and at such an early age provide keys to his character outside of the kind of honing of his gunfighter skills usual in a story about a boy's coming of age.

Susan

Susan Delgado is the daughter of Patrick, manager of the Major's horses. Susan learns during the course of the story that her father was betrayed by those who would join with Farson because of his allegiance to the Affiliation. As she gains knowledge of her past and experiences love, she develops as a character. The flashback opens with her trip to Rhea for proof of her virginity and ends after her death. From the innocent young girl of the beginning she becomes a strong young woman who assists Roland and is pregnant with his child. She dies because she is betrayed by her aunt and her town and because Roland believes the magic ball when he sees Susan captured but alive. She contributes to the success of Roland's plans, but she cannot survive. She is his great love, but in the world of the series, the gunslinger must ride alone. The plot of the novel dictates both her love and her death.

Eldred Jonas

Eldred Jonas is the leader of the Big Coffin Hunters. At first he is presented as the most intelligent and skilled member of this group. But there are early suggestions that his character has greater depth. His long mustache is seen as a "sham gunslinger's mustache" (172) by many who would never suggest such a thing directly to him. This early association with gunslingers is a hint of the real connection that Roland uncovers later. His ability as a leader and planner has its source in his background. When Jonas captures Roland, the young man realizes that Jonas is a failed gunfighter because the training never really leaves a man.

Roland knows that Jonas has been exiled from Gilead, a dropout as a gunslinger. Jonas has been exiled by Fardo, the father of Cort, whom Roland defeated to become a gunslinger. Jonas is really a foil for Roland; his failures are Roland's successes. Even Jonas's love affair with Coral, the sister of the mayor, mirrors Roland's relationship with the future mistress of the mayor, Susan. Jonas and Coral enjoy a love of evil and of wild sex but none of the shared purpose that unites Susan and Roland. The magic ball seduces Jonas, but he is forced to give it up to Roland just before the young gunslinger kills him. His failure in life extends to his death.

THEME

While King amplifies the themes associated with the Dark Tower series, such as the importance of ecology, the father-son relationship, connections between people, and the role of fate, the complex structure of *Wizard and Glass* adds other themes: the fragility of the real world, the fluctuations possible in time, and the influence of the past on the present. The complex structure of the framing story and the flashback provides much of the interaction of the themes. King's growing interest in different ideas over the long course of time he has taken to write the volumes in this series is another reason for the increasing thematic complexity of this novel. Just as nothing in the worlds of this series remains static, so the various ideas expressed in these works are constantly shifting. The overriding image from all of the worlds is that of the Dark Tower. Roland sees that the Tower is crumbling, and its fall would mean the end of the known world (581). The Tower is both a place of strength and the source of the slippage between the various worlds: "this jutting arm of dark gray stone is the world's great mystery and last awful riddle" (572). All of the themes are reflected in the quest for the Tower and the solutions to its mysteries.

The land in the series is constantly under threat. Sometimes the ravages it has endured are greater than others. In the opening of the novel, as they ride the train, Roland, Susannah, Eddie, and Jake catch brief glimpses of a world that is healing. Both flora and fauna seem to be returning to normal. The same healing is visible in Mejis. While the witch Rhea's cat dangles extra legs, more horses are being bred true to their lines. However, behind the positive signs, the thinny grows in both the flashback and the framing story. It represents both a physical and a spiritual evil, places where the decaying force of the Tower can no longer prevent the erosion of the fabric of existence (66). Roland is able to use the thinny to destroy the Good Man's army in the flashback, but the friends of his youth are almost pulled into it as well. Once Roland and his *ka-tet* hit the turnpike in the framing story they must fight to ignore it when it borders the highway.

If the land Roland sees while riding on the train has improved slightly, the world he and his friends enter once it crashes has suffered another assault. They have broken through into the world of *The Stand*, where a different kind of man-made disaster has killed most of human life. As they pass through the city and onto the highway, Eddie, Susannah, and Jake observe the decay of a world similar to the ones they have left. Now they are able to share Roland's perception of the impending ruin if they are not successful in their pursuit of the Dark Tower. The interaction of the two stories deepens their appreciation of the importance of Roland's choice to abandon everything else for this one goal.

The interaction of framing and flashback stories brings a bit more understanding of parent-child relationships to Jake. As he listens to Roland's story and even views it in the glass, Jake realizes how his own parents, Elmer and Megan Chambers, resemble Steven and Gabrielle Deschain. Both fathers are gunslingers in their respective worlds, and both mothers have been unfaithful. But he also sees that Roland's mother had planned to kill her husband because she was so in love with Marten, the magician. Other parent-child relationships reflect these two in the novel. Susan constantly considers what her father might have thought if he had been alive. Her aunt's betrayal of Patrick is a version of the betrayal of basic family ties that signals a disintegration in the operation of the world.

A more positive version of the family is depicted in the way the rest of the *ka-tet* interacts with Jake. While he is a full participant in their activities, they still are aware of his youth and often assume the role of absent parent. The members of the *ka-tet* also help Roland reconcile himself with the killing of his mother and the way his father might have contributed to this horrible act by not challenging fate.

In addition to the actual parent-child relationships depicted in *Wizard and Glass*, there are metaphoric representations of this kind of interpersonal connection. The reason boys give for their being sent to Mejis involves their fathers. The Coffin Hunters ignore them for a while because they are just boys. These men have never had sons and do not understand how families operate. In a sense the Roland of the flashback has become his father in the framing story, the person he could never please. And the concept behind *The Wizard of Oz* is of a return to family. Unlike Susan, Dorothy has a positive connection to her aunt. Many of these stories are of surrogate parents. In a world of shifting realities even the idea of the nuclear family is unstable.

The connections between people are just as fragile as those within the family in *Wizard and Glass*. The concept of the *ka-tet* is continued and amplified in this novel. Toward the end Roland realizes he must reveal everything about his earlier life if he is to continue with these people. In order to be a group united by fate he had to show them the hidden shame of his killing of his mother. Roland is a member of two *ka-tets* in the novel, and the flashback reveals the trouble in the earlier one. In the previous works in the series King shows how each individual becomes a member of the group. In the flashback the young men are already part of a group, but their youth and inexperience reveal the fragility of their connection to each other. While Susan does become a part of the *ka-tet*, she also reveals its stress.

The love between Susan and Roland threatens the group. On two occasions one of the other members of the group has to hit Roland to get him to turn from his love to his duty. The events at the end of the novel even call into question the effectiveness of such a group. King does not reveal what happens to Alain and Cuthbert, but there is a suggestion of death and betrayal. And even though the young men do defeat a portion of Farson's army, they only delay the defeat of the Alliance. But membership in a *ka-tet* is certainly more positive than any other kind of societal connection in this novel. The Coffin Hunters do not survive as a group. After Jonas's death Coral forms a relationship with Reynolds until they are killed. The Coffin Hunters betray those who think they are a part of the group, like the mayor and the Chancellor, Kimba Rimer. While members of the *ka-tet* must deal with the role of fate in their lives, those who do not form such relationships must face the relentless working out of destiny without the support of others.

The action of *ka* in the lives of individuals and groups is important in the Dark Tower series and in other King novels. This word, which can best be identified with the idea of fate, remains constant, but its working in the lives of the characters is developed more fully each time it appears. Susan sees her attraction to Roland as *ka*, a force that her father has explained is both dangerous and inevitable. It can bring pleasure, but it can also destroy. She understands that the real challenge is to identify its presence and not use desire as an excuse for *ka*. She must decide whether her love is really fate or just the wishing that it were. In *Wizard and Glass* the operation of *ka* is further complicated by the presence of the Maerlyn's Glass, part of the great wizard's Rainbow. Many of the pieces have been broken. They all provide a kind of vision—the future, the present, hidden secrets, or even the location of secret doors between worlds. They never show the good in the world, and Steven warns Roland about the pink glass in the hand of Farson that can show events in the present, past, or future.

The problem with such a talisman is that the user becomes used by it, absorbed by it. By showing Roland the decaying tower and hiding Susan's fate until too late, the glass gives him information that makes him choose the tower over his love. Those absorbed by the glass have to face limited options rather than the complex working of *ka*. At the end of the novel Susannah expresses a different appreciation of *ka* when she declares that she would rather live in a world with it than in a world without it. The experience with the Wizard's Glass shows Roland and his group that is it better not to see too far into what might be because such knowledge is evil. It is better to act according to one's principles in a world governed by *ka*.

Following one's *ka* is even more difficult when one is faced with an ever shifting reality. While King exposes the fragility of our perception of the real world in many of his novels, the characters in the Dark Tower series are constantly confronting situations that challenge their sense of the orderly operation of the universe. Eddie, Susannah, and Jake have passed through doors from their worlds to Roland's. In *Wizard and Glass* they already understand the concept of parallel existences, but they see a new version of this idea when they enter a Kansas that is like the world they left but also different from it. Roland is the one who most fully understands the instability of the realities he has experienced. The fusion of various worlds happens because of the weakening of the tower. But through their learning of the events of the flashback, Eddie, Susannah, and Jake also experience the thinness of reality.

Their understanding of the fragility of reality is connected to the shifting operation of time in these unstable worlds. Roland's story only takes one night to tell, and when he has finished they do not even feel tired. But they know it should have taken much longer. On the train, Blaine's time is also different from theirs. In the flashback time seems to be contained by its connection to the flow of the seasons. But even in a world governed by the necessities of nature people begin to feel something is wrong. They are at the end of an era; their world will be destroyed with the coming defeat of the Affiliation. As King presents it, "Time is a face on the water" (447). The flashback is constructed according to the concept of parallel actions as it moves from one group of characters to another. But by the end of the story, shifts in time reflect underlying forces moving the various worlds and challenging reality.

The interactions of past and present are yet another aspect of the elaborate connections among time, reality, and the ever shifting universe of the novel. In a conventional sense Roland must make peace with his past and understand it if he and his *ka-tet* are to progress. The structure of the novel into framing story and flashback would suggest an orderly connection between past and present. But the changing worlds the characters encounter compress all of their experiences. They enter into the Wizard's Glass and share an event from Roland's past. He sees into the future. A parallel world makes a mockery of their past experiences because their memories are challenged by things they have never seen.

Roland's past exists in many different worlds. They can, to a certain extent, trust the experiences they have shared. But ultimately *Wizard and Glass* leaves them with only one certainty: the quest for the Dark Tower that lies on the Path of the Beam.

ALTERNATIVE READING: READER RESPONSE THEORY

Reader response theory deals with the relationship between the reader and the text. In this approach the critic looks both at the way a text directs the reader and the way a reader interacts with the text. Meaning is generated by this exchange and is not static. Each encounter with the text can create a different reading because of the unique experiences each person brings to this encounter. Texts are constructed to elicit responses. The narrative is organized to create questions that can only be answered by continuing to read. People want to know what happens next and why it happens. Before such questions are answered the reader may either fill in the gaps with her or his own solutions or wait in suspense for the answers. In popular genres, the genre form provides the reader with clues as to how to experience the text. In a mystery the reader knows that the story will end with the solution of the crime. In a western she or he expects a final confrontation between the good and evil characters, a certain kind of setting, and the use of guns and horses. The kind of response a reader gives is also conditioned by previous experience with a genre, but even someone new to a genre should be able to pick up some of its conventions, the unstated rules that organize it. The author has to write both for the experienced reader and the novice. In the Dark Tower series, King faces an even greater challenge because he writes both for the dedicated fan who knows the series and for the newcomer who is encountering this work for the first time.

King helps both types of readers at the beginning of *Wizard and Glass* with his summary of the events of the preceding novels in the series. He then opens the book with a resumption of the conflict with Blaine that ended the previous volume. Old and new readers are quickly drawn into the story. If one is encountering old friends, the clues about character and genre only serve to renew the pleasures of the series. The new reader uses these clues as a means of differentiating the characters and putting together further elements in their histories.

As the characters leave Blaine for the next part of the story, the reader is engaged by information that suggests the direction of the narrative.

The arrival in Kansas in a novel with "wizard" in its title hints at associations with Dorothy and Toto. At the same time King draws readers into the narrative that will become the main story in the book through Roland's short flashback when they first encounter the noise made by the thinny. The suggestions of things to come provide the questions that drive the narrative for the reader. In addition, in this early section of the novel King's inclusion of elements of *The Stand* gives the knowledgeable reader a different kind of experience with the work. While King is ahead of the reader and the characters with suggestions of things to come, the experienced King reader is ahead of the characters in understanding references to other King novels.

Generic conventions are most important when Roland begins the story told in the flashback. The use of various kinds of moons as titles immediately suggests a rural community with close ties to the seasons. The introduction of the witch and tests for virginity gives the reader clues about a world with quite different standards from that of the modern Kansas of the framing story. Since King combines elements of the Arthurian legend, an epic fantasy, with the western, the language and details of setting immediately give clues to this mixture. Men ride horses, there are references to canyons, and a man is both mayor and involved in a barony. All of these terms provide elements of the genres that any reader familiar with popular culture should be able to understand.

In addition to the use of genre as a means of engaging the reader with the novel, King constantly hints at actions to come. Rather than reducing suspense, these clues pull the reader further into the novel because they raise new questions. Since Susan does not appear in any other novels in the series, the reader would not be surprised to find out that she does not survive in *Wizard and Glass*. The hints King provides about her only serve to raise questions about what will happen each time she seems to escape from danger. For the reader familiar with the series, the introduction of a young Roland allows for a new understanding of the formation of his character. King includes references to the mature Roland as well so that even the newcomer can put together past and present for an understanding of the formation of this man.

The end of the novel involves the reader with another kind of experience. Once King returns to the framing story, he gradually provides resolutions for unanswered questions from the flashback at the same time that he uses the Oz story to reintroduce Roland's larger quest for the beam. He must resolve the Susan story and at the same time generate new questions to maintain interest in the next volume in the Dark Tower series. King's final revelations about Roland's mother's death bring an end to that era in this character's life. The experiences Roland's group has in the Emerald Palace renew their concern with the search for the Dark Tower that is the real focus of the series.

By the end of the novel King has involved the reader in the complex process of finding resolution for this particular work while maintaining suspense about the ultimate outcome of the quest. Reader response theory helps the critic trace the ways the text is organized to incorporate the reader in the experience with the work. It can also suggest areas of individual response to a given work based on the reader's awareness of the structures governing it. This approach can demonstrate how a novel in a series can both continue to involve the reader and create anticipation for the next volume, while presenting a satisfying experience with the current one.

6

Bag of Bones
(1998)

In *Bag of Bones* Stephen King returns to familiar locations, favorite themes, and an author as a central character, but in this novel he brings a maturity to these subjects that marks much of his recent work. The title refers to the human body, especially the dead body, and leads the reader to one of its central concepts: the ways that the literal and figurative ghosts of the past haunt the present. The presence of ghosts recalls such works as *The Shining*, but in *Bag of Bones* both the ghosts and their motivations are much more complex than in the earlier novel.

This book opens in Derry, which is a well-known King location, the site of such works as *Dreamcatcher*, *Insomnia* and *It*, and moves to Dark Score Lake in western Maine, also familiar territory, but again presented with a difference. The name of the lake reverberates through the novel, where many forces struggle to even up "dark scores" from the past. Michael Noonan, the central character and narrator, is an author, like Thad Beaumont of *The Dark Half*. But rather than dealing with the relationship between author and creation or author and fan, as he has in other books, King concentrates on the act of writing, the connection between real and fictional worlds, and the morality of the very act of presenting products of the imagination. The novel is full of references to other works. One of Thad Beaumont's novels keeps Michael Noonan off the best-seller list. At one point Mike asks where Sheriff Alan Pangborn and his wife are (*The Dark Half*, *Needful Things*). Mike receives a helpful suggestion from a retired man who lives in Derry. Mike feels the man shares his own inability to sleep. The man is Ralph Roberts of *Insomnia*. In *Bag of Bones* King too returns to his own literary history in order to reevaluate it and reflect on it.

The novel's three epigraphs illustrate King's acknowledgment of a literary past, one that also haunts this work. The first quotation is from "Bartleby" by Herman Melville and connects King's considerations of the role of the author with the love story. The second, from *Rebecca* by Daphne du Maurier, introduces the concepts of the past haunting the present and the importance of place. The third, Ray Bradbury's single sentence, "Mars is heaven," deals with characterization of some of the inhabitants of the land around Dark Score Lake, an unincorporated area appearing on the map as TR-90 and known to those who live there as the TR. The range of fictional elements covered by these epigraphs is another gauge of the complexity of the novel. Setting, plot, and character are related to these phrases. They introduce the basic elements of the novel and suggest its themes and at the same time indicate its range of interests.

PLOT DEVELOPMENT

King unites structure and theme in his organization of the plot in *Bag of Bones*. He presents the story as a first-person narrative told from the point of view of the central character, Michael Noonan. As a first-person narrative usually deals with what has been—the character retells a story that has already happened—the plot must deal with the past rather than with what is happening in the present. *Bag of Bones* is a narrative about several kinds of pasts and the way events from a distant era can direct the present. Ghosts haunt the story, and the plot reflects those ghosts in its organization through strands that appear, disappear, and finally reappear and connect.

The novel opens with a shock, the death of Mike's wife. This event is set firmly in time: "On a very hot day in August of 1994, my wife told me she was going down to the Derry Rite Aid. . . . The next time I saw her was on TV" (1). He sees her on TV because that is how the dead are identified in Derry. He then carefully reconstructs the last moments of her life. As he recounts the details of this event he adds some words that serve as a narrative device throughout the novel. He describes finding a surprise among her purchases—an item he does not immediately identify—and says he does not think she may have been leading another life: "Not then" (2). With those words he sends the reader forward into the story. We are alerted to possibilities that will happen. At this point we do not know what or when. King uses this device to hook us into the story and pull us along. While we may assume that Mike has survived the events of the novel, since he is telling the story, these hooks placed throughout the narration generate suspense and keep the reader involved in guessing what might be ahead. King structures the novel by carefully controlling the flow of information to the reader. While *Bag of Bones* is a ghost story, it is also a mystery. Just as Mike organizes how he reveals information, so King doles out the clues to the solution of the central mystery, forcing Mike to act as a detective. But unlike those of traditional mystery, the solutions to Mike's questions lie hidden in a past that can only be reached by supernatural rather than natural means.

King also structures the opening to establish a pattern of misdirection that will involve the reader. From Mike's description of his wife's death we are led to believe she somehow is killed in the accident he so vividly describes, but Johanna Arlen Noonan dies from a brain aneurysm as she runs toward the car crash. Gradually in this opening King reveals small details that only establish new questions. We learn that the strange object Johanna purchased was a pregnancy test, and she was indeed pregnant with a girl who would have been called Kia Jane. But it is not until near the end of the novel that we finally understand why she has hidden this possible pregnancy from her husband. She does not want to bear a child who will be subject to evil reprisals from events that occurred long ago. The question of her secret life introduced at this point is what impels Mike's interest in the past. But the novel is not just a voyage into history. Johanna's death has serious implications for the present that also affect the novel's organization.

At the moment King seems to point the reader toward the possibility of Johanna's now-ongoing ghostly presence, the connection to the past, he shifts the direction of the book toward Mike's current problems. Mike is a successful author who is finishing a novel. After he completes his book he finds he can no longer write. He is a victim of such a complete writer's block that he becomes ill if he even attempts to use the computer to write fiction. This problem becomes the second narrative strand of the complex plot of *Bag of Bones*.

King continues to alternate descriptions of the problems generated by this block with Mike's memories of his wife. Both of these plot elements become associated with places in Maine. Mike and Jo have two homes—the large winter house in Derry and the summer lodge on Dark Score Lake called "Sara Laughs." For some reason Jo and Mike have not spent the summer of her death at the lake even though he has written there in the past. Both the writer's block and Johanna's continued presence after her death are, at first, associated with the house in Derry. But even in this home Sara Laughs invades Mike's dreams. When Mike is finally able to return to the lake he encounters the third plot element.

Mike suddenly sees a young child walking down the middle of the road. She is Kyra Devore, daughter of Mattie and granddaughter of Max Devore. Mike rescues Kyra from the road and becomes involved in the custody battle between her widowed mother and her wealthy grandfather. This third strand of the story ultimately provides the connections to the two other plot lines. At first Mike only sees Kyra, whose name bears a close resemblance to the one that he and Jo had chosen if they were to have had a daughter. When he is drawn into the custody battle, he learns of his more complicated relationship to Max Devore—a link discovered by Johanna before her death. King gradually weaves this strand, which at first seems separate from the others, into the plot. Even though it is introduced last, it becomes the force that impels the plot toward its resolution. Mike's ancestors are connected to an evil event precipitated by Max's great-grandfather.

Bag of Bones ends with a series of upheavals in the natural and supernatural worlds. The three strands are joined when the past erupts into the present. All are touched by the depraved events that haunt the TR. Johanna's ghost leads Mike to a solution of the mystery surrounding his own ancestors and the evil spirits they have generated. She controls him so that the writer's block he thinks he has overcome is really a means for her to reveal the place where she has hidden her research into the past. Through Jo's tracing of Mike's family tree he understands his connection to Max and the underlying reason for his attraction to Kyra. The rape of Sara Tidwell and her murder and that of her son and her nephew, crimes committed by Max and his friends in the distant past, haunt their descendants. As the action accelerates, King increases his use of the foreshadowing plot hooks that he established in the beginning.

By this point the reader is aware of their importance. Rather than diffusing the impact of the events, King's foreshadowing amplifies the reader's anxiety. When we learn of Mattie's impending death, we can hardly wait to turn the pages to find out how and why it occurs. At the same time we do not want to know; we do not want to read the words that detail her death. We can see how the different plots are inevitably coming together, and we want to know the answer to their mysteries. But we do not want to face the horror that must accompany the resolution. In *Bag of Bones* King has constructed a complex plot where the three stories and their related themes are united at the end with such force that no real peaceful resolution is possible. Mike can only contain the forces released by Sara Tidwell's desire for revenge.

The novel ends with an epilogue. Usually King's epilogues show how the characters find ways to return to some kind of resolution of the problems raised during the course of the novel. While the ending of *Bag of Bones* suggests some hope for the future, the recovery will take longer and be less complete than in some of the other King novels. Secondary characters will carry physical and mental scars. Mike may eventually be allowed to adopt Kyra, but he will never return to writing fiction; he has found reality too powerful and too tragic to be transformed into fiction. While King demonstrates his skill as a writer in the way he unites structure and theme in this novel, he ends by having his central character question the value of fiction.

CHARACTER DEVELOPMENT

King's approach to his characters is unusual in *Bag of Bones* because he has constructed the novel as a first-person narrative. Since we see everything through Mike Noonan's eyes, he dominates the story. The first-person narrative also alters the relationship between character and plot. While the plot usually dominates King's fictional world, Mike's personal and professional problems are central to this book in the same way that Dolores Claiborne's character controls the novel with her name. In addition to the focus on the presentation of the narrator, the novel combines traditional characters with complexly developed ghosts. Unlike the ghosts in *The Shining*, these figures in *Bag of Bones* come from near and distant pasts and are either good or mixtures of good and evil. All of the characters, both living and dead, function in relation to Mike Noonan. Johanna, Mike's dead wife, exists both in flashback and in her ghostly acts during the course of the novel. Mattie and Kyra Devore, mother and daughter, are the most important of the living characters. Max Devore represents evil from the present with strong ties to the past. Sara Tidwell is a ghost from the past who haunts the story and comes to life in a flashback that provides the solution to the major mystery.

Michael Noonan

As the narrator of the novel, Mike Noonan reveals himself to the reader. The most important aspects of his personality appear early in the novel and are gradually amplified through its plot. We first see him as he recounts the events leading to the death of his wife, Johanna. At the time of her death in August 1994, Mike is thirty-six and his wife thirty-four. They have been married for ten years. In addition to his role as grieving widower, Mike also quickly presents the reader with the other formative aspect of his character: he is a successful writer. He links his marriage to his career. His wife's actions, her approval of his first novel, and the ritual they develop at the completion of a work are central to his writing. His wife's death and his writer's block form the basis of all of the early revelations about his character.

At first Mike defines himself through his writing. But as he learns just how severe and seemingly final his inability to write has become, he must develop new resources in order to survive. While he is finishing the novel he has been writing at the time of Johanna's death, he explains his status as a novelist. He has made a lot of money—enough to own two homes and have a good life. Mike has never had a best-seller, but one book reached number five on the *New York Times* best-seller list. He discovers that any attempt to write creates a violent physical reaction when he begins a new work. He is unable to confess this problem to his publisher and, instead, sends his agent books he has stockpiled during more prolific times.

Here Mike mirror's King's experiences with publishing. Publishers want to maintain a steady demand for authors' works and will often not allow them to publish more than one book a year even though they can write more. In King's case he got around this restriction by publishing under the name Richard Bachman. Mike has put his novels away in his safe-deposit box. By withdrawing one a year, he can maintain the fiction that he is still writing for his agent and publisher. When he sends in the final book, Mike realizes that he must confront elements of his existence. The end of the stockpile of books from the past forces Mike to return to other aspects of his life and eventually discover an unknown family history that connects him to unsuspected evil.

Mike realizes he must face fears represented by recurring dreams and leave his house in Derry for the summer home, Sara Laughs. His writer's personality emerges even in his dreams, where his return to Sara Laughs is associated with the famous opening of Daphne du Maurier's *Rebecca* when the narrator dreams of returning to Manderley. Just as Manderley is haunted by ghosts, so is Mike's house. But the events Mike confronts when he returns to Sara Laughs become the ultimate test of his character. In the first half of the novel he passively accepts what is happening; in the second half he fights back, both for himself and for others. He takes on Mattie Devore's custody fight with her father-in-law, Max, over Kyra, and he follows Johanna's ghostly leads in investigating a horrible series of events from the past that dominate the present. Through these struggles he acts as a detective uncovering the community's secrets, and he suffers another death of a loved one, Mattie. By the end of the novel Mike realizes that some losses can never be recovered. The love of Kyra, a kind of daughter, sustains him, but the deaths of her mother and of Mike's wife lead him to understand that reality is too violent to be represented through fiction. Mike decides he cannot write. He recalls what Thomas Hardy states in *Jude the Obscure*—that the best fictional character was just a bag of bones. As Hardy found fiction useless when compared to the real world, so Mike makes the same discovery. In an irony formulated by King, who does not suffer from writer's block and who continues to write, Mike decides that contributing to the real world is more important than playing in a fictional one.

Johanna Noonan

King presents Johanna Noonan in a very interesting manner: she is dead before the novel begins. We only experience her personality as her husband recalls events from the past or as she appears as a ghost. After the description of her death and the revelation that she had just secretly purchased a pregnancy test, the first part of the novel deals with her connection to Mike. It is after he returns to their summer home that more of her private life is revealed. Her ghost begins to direct Mike in a variety of ways. She manifests herself as the force ringing the bell on Bunter, the stuffed moose, in response to his questions. As the reader eventually learns, she also writes Mike's new novel as a way of attempting to lead him to important clues about both his past and that of others around Dark Score Lake.

Johanna operates as a spiritual presence and as a collection of her artifacts from the past. Both elements guide Mike. Many of the things she has created are visual, such as her photography and the various crafts projects she explored. But much of her contact with Mike as a ghost is through the written word, an acceptance of her husband's world. She arranges the magnetic letters on the refrigerator into words and cryptic messages. The new novel she writes with him on the old typewriter she has appropriated is really an elaborate series of clues to the hiding place for detective work she has already done. At first Jo only manifests herself through the movement of inanimate objects. But toward the end of the

novel she becomes an active combatant in the fight against Sara and the
evil forces she has released. The notes she has left lead Mike to an understanding of the central mystery of Dark Score Lake and his relationship to the perpetrators.

Jo's research reveals that Mike's great-grandfather's sister had married
Benton Auster. The child of this union is one of the group of men who
rape and kill Sara Tidwell and later kill her son because he saw them.
Johanna's interest in the past stems from her realization that she may be
pregnant, and she knows she must solve the mystery to save the life of
her future child from Sara's revenge. She dies before she can reveal to
Mike what she has learned about the past because he is too involved in
writing his novel. But she returns as a ghost to help him set the past to
rest so that their surrogate child, Kyra, can survive. One of the first messages she forms on the refrigerator is a request for Mike to help Mattie.

Mattie and Kyra Devore

Mattie and her daughter Kyra come into the novel and into Mike's life
through an event that is firmly based in a frightening encounter in the
real world. It is only later that their connection to the past and the world
of ghosts is revealed. The first morning of his return to the TR, Mike is
on his way to lunch when sees a little girl walking down the middle of
the highway. Mike rescues her from her march to the beach on the center
white line. When her mother arrives, desperately looking for her, both
Mattie and Kyra begin a relationship with Mike that transforms all of
their lives. For the young child there is an immediate psychic bond with
Mike. As the story progresses they share the ability to see the ghosts and
return to the past with them because they share blood bonds to these
distant events.

Mattie is a twenty-one-year-old widow who is fighting her wealthy
father-in-law for custody of Kyra. At first Mike thinks she's just another
trailer-trash mom, but he soon discovers the depth of her love for Kyra
and those qualities that extend beyond his first impression of a beautiful
young woman in a Kmart smock. Mike is not simply drawn to both of
them because Kyra's name is so close to Kia, the name he and Jo had
chosen for their child. He decides to help with the custody battle, and
gradually Mattie falls in love with him and he with her. Mattie met Lance
Devore, Max's son, when he was twenty-one and she was seventeen. She
had a hard childhood, and life did not get easier with her marriage
because Lance's father disapproved. When Lance is killed falling off a

ladder during a lightning storm, she is left alone with her father-in-law, who claims she is an unfit mother.

The relationship between Mattie and Mike develops when she invites him to dinner and they discuss Herman Melville's "Bartleby," which Mattie is reading for a book discussion group. Mike explains Bartleby as someone who begins to question everything in life. He has only his work, and when he questions that he loses all connection to the world. Their discussion of the story reveals Mattie's intelligence, involvement with life, and excitement about ideas.

Max Devore

Mike first encounters Max the night after he meets Mattie and Kyra. Max is an extremely wealthy old man who has made his money in the computer software business. While he comes from the TR, he no longer lives there. He has returned to the region to fight for custody of Kyra. Max's character is defined by an action in his youth. He had badly cut his hands breaking into a shed to get a sled another boy had received for Christmas. He was found on the hill with blood all over his mittens and snowsuit, but he had been using the sled. Max stops at nothing to get what he wants. He even arranges for Mattie's death after his own. Jared Devore, his great-grandfather, was the leader of the group of men who attacked Sara Tidwell and her son, setting off the ghostly events of *Bag of Bones*. Max, who stays alive only with the help of his crazy daughter and an oxygen tank, is the most literal manifestation of the title of the novel.

Sara Tidwell

Sara Tidwell, an African American, is the most famous member of the Tidwell family. She is the lead singer in the group known as Sara and the Red-Tops and the source of the name of Mike's summer home, Sara Laughs. But Sara also embodies an attitude, an approach to life that infuriates some of the inhabitants of the area around Dark Score Lake. During the summer of 1901 she and her family are extremely popular entertainers. In a period when the Civil War is still an active memory for some, her easy relationship with the Euro-Americans who live along the lake angers people because she expects to be treated as an equal and is by some. It is her laugh that seems to make her so attractive to those she meets, but this laugh also precipitates her rape and death. She cannot help laughing when the irate group of men confronts her and, when led by Jared Devore, rape her and eventually kill her and her son. Even though they bury her, Sara does not rest. She is the ghost who returns to destroy the children of the men who killed her. Kyra is the last of those children, and Mike, with Jo's help, must fight her to save the young girl. Sara's hatred has transformed her. She has become one of the Outsiders, who are very dangerous. Mike obliterates her bones and those of her son. Sara is finally destroyed and her ghost rests, but the Outsider still lurks, waiting for the bags of bones each person represents.

THEMES

There are complex connections among the four major themes in *Bag of Bones*. The novel investigates the role of the author, the interaction of fiction and reality, the influence of the past on the present, and the importance of all aspects of love in the family (husband/wife, parent/child, brothers-in-law). Both the positive and negative aspects of all of these themes are central to the book. Mike, the narrator, is the character who finally unites the four major themes as he recounts its events to his brother-in-law, Frank Arlen. King's skill in the construction of this novel is evident in the way the complexity of its form reflects the interaction of the themes as it moves between past and present, reality and a ghostly past.

The novel begins and ends with family. It opens with the story of Johanna's death and ends with an epilogue that reveals how Mike has been telling the entire story to Frank. He also relates his efforts to adopt Kyra. The bonds of love have saved Mike and Kyra from destruction and provide the only hope for the future. The family love shared by Frank and Mike helps Mike survive difficult times. Johanna's love also saves Mike at a critical point in the narrative. Mattie's ghost saves her daughter. Mattie's marriage has created Kyra, who is the hope for the future. But her marriage to Lance sets in motion the backlash of Max, the evil father-in-law. He uses his daughter, Rogette Whitmore, to attempt to destroy Kyra and is successful in having Mattie killed. Frank's relationship with his sister leads to a moment when a story about his helping her leads Mike to think she may have been involved in an affair. Mike hears of a strange man with Johanna at a ball game and only learns much later that the man was Frank.

Johanna's love has also led her to an investigation of the past that reveals what happens when family love is distorted by hatred. She discovers the family connections to the men who killed Sara, her son, and eventually her nephew, Reg Tidwell, Jr. These deaths lead to the transformation of love into hatred as Sara seeks revenge. She returns from the past to eliminate the families of those who destroyed her and hers. King suggests that family relations generate powerful feelings that can operate for good or be transformed into evil.

Sara also provides the focus for the thematic connections between past and present. Her ghost forces the descendants of those who wronged her to face the legacy of the past. Johanna also returns from a more immediate past to lead Mike to an understanding of the legacy of hatred that haunts this area of Maine. But the events of years ago have broader implications for the novel. Sara's death is linked to a larger concern for the history of race relations in the United States. She and her family are punished for daring to think they are just like their neighbors. Because their music has given them a measure of acceptance, they make the mistake of thinking racial prejudice no longer exists in this part of the country. The local inhabitants have not forgotten their prejudices. They have not let go of the past, the Civil War, and its aftermath. While the summer visitors from more sophisticated locales socialize with the Tidwells, times have not really changed in this corner of western Maine. In fact, turn of the century attitudes haunt the present. Rather than Jared Devore, the leader of the gang that killed Sara, the current citizens of the TR are under the influence of Max. The house that bears her name, Sara Laughs, provides another conduit to the past. It was her laughter that ultimately provoked her death. In the house the ghosts of Sara and Johanna fight to control Mike and Kyra. The house also links the past to other themes— reality versus fiction and the world of the author.

The presence of ghosts calls into question what is real and what is imagined. For Mike, an author, the connection between what actually happened and what he thought might have happened is even more tenuous. He constantly acknowledges that his working life has been spent creating imaginary worlds. When his dreams come alive at Sara Laughs, he begins to question what is real. His perception of the world is further colored by his experiences with other writers. His dreams about returning to Sara Laughs are recounted in the context of Daphne du Maurier's description of Rebecca's return to Manderley in the novel that bears her name. Rebecca, too, must deal with a house that is haunted by evil secrets. She imagines relationships that differ greatly from reality.

Mike has spent his whole life balancing between his experiences and his transformation of life into fiction. In addition to the ghosts who actually appear in his life, he must deal with all of the characters he has created. His involvement with his writing led Johanna to attempt to solve the mysteries of Sara Laughs on her own. He finds he can no longer write once he finishes that novel. The alternate world of fiction becomes the too real invasion of ghosts into everyday life. To survive, Mike has to believe in a world most of us only encounter in fiction. Even the novel he thinks he is writing is actually created by a ghost, Johanna, as a means of using his fiction to show him the path to the ghostly reality of the past.

All of the themes are finally united in the concept of the world of the author. If Mike is the narrator who recounts all of the events of the novel and questions the connections between fiction and reality, King is the author who stands behind the novel. The knowledgeable reader is always aware of his presence. King, the prolific author, writes a story of a man suffering from writer's block. King, the man dedicated to fiction, creates a character who ends up rejecting the form because reality is too horrible to be transformed into a novel. King, the genre writer, uses examples from Thomas Hardy and Herman Melville, authors known for fiction that is usually set against popular genre works, to develop his ideas. Mike rejects the writing of fiction because of his experiences and what he has learned from Hardy and Melville. He takes from Hardy the idea that the most carefully constructed character is nothing more than a bag of bones when compared to a real person. Melville's Bartleby was one of the first characters he discussed with Mattie. At the end of the novel he puts down his pen like the scrivener who makes decisions because he prefers not to do something. Mike prefers not to write. But King obviously does not share Mike's view of the world of fiction. It is a measure of the depth of the novel that King can convincingly present a character who challenges the very work that is central to his own existence.

Bag of Bones is one of King's most complex novels. In this book he provides a mature version of many of the themes he has explored in earlier works, such as parent/child and husband/wife relationships, the role of the author, and the influence of an evil past. But in *Bag of Bones* all of these themes are united. Rather than the simple evil of earlier novels, the world of this novel is inhabited by ghosts who have suffered real wrongs. King shows the reader that good and evil are motivated by people with complex desires. The characters in this novel are reflections of the tangled motivations that animate people in the real world. They are more than bags of bones, but King also shows the reader the world behind the fictional façade of his novel. Reality is always more horrible than fiction. Mike sees this truth and can no longer write. King presents this truth but does not abandon the attempt to breathe life into these bones.

ALTERNATIVE READING: MEN'S STUDIES

Men's studies is a relatively new area in literary criticism. It is an outgrowth of developments in feminist and queer studies, approaches that deal directly with the analysis of gender and sexual orientation in all aspects of society. Men's studies turns this focus to issues of masculinity and deals with the analysis of male roles in artistic works. In men's studies, depictions of masculinity are seen as part of an ever changing response to the diversity of representations of males in society. Feminist studies and queer studies have led to an understanding of the ways that our comprehension of the role of gender exists as a social construction. There is not just one way to view gender in our society, and our perception of gender is, to a great extent, the result of concepts imposed by society. As society alters the roles assigned to gender, our concept of the roles of men and women changes. Recent King novels demonstrate how his view of women has developed over the course of his career. Both *Dolores Claiborne* and *Rose Madder* deal with feminist issues. In *Bag of Bones* King turns his attention to the role of men in late twentieth-century society.

Mike is a man who is willing to reveal his weaknesses as well as his strengths, just as a man's ability to reveal the fears behind the strong façade expected by society is an indication of changing views of male roles examined in men's studies. From the opening of the novel Mike admits to Frank that he has trouble asking other people for help. But later he is able to talk to his brother-in-law about the loss of Johanna. Even though Mike cannot reveal the secret of his writer's block, he does accept Frank's invitation to visit during the first Christmas after Johanna's death and grieve with the rest of her family.

The novel ends at yet another Christmas celebration. This time Mike tells Frank the entire story of the events that form the novel, revealing all of his strengths and weaknesses. Throughout the novel Frank and Mike discuss topics not associated with typical male conversations, stereotyped as confined to sports and descriptions or triumphs in business and personal lives. Frank even brings up the topic of sex with Mike, who admits he has not had relations with another woman since Johanna's death. These kinds of personal revelations lead to an image of masculinity that acknowledges a range of roles usually absent from the more action-oriented heroes of genre fiction.

The changing role of the father is another aspect of the depiction of males that is central to men's studies. While Mike can be seen as another in the long line of fathers in King's novels with either natural or surrogate children, both his character and his relationship with the child are more complexly presented. Mike's psychic bond with Kyra leads him to protect her, but he must also fight the inherited impulse to destroy her. On a larger scale these warring forces acknowledge the real conflicts parents must face rather than idealized views of parent/child relationships. Mike even recognizes how society might view his initial encounter with Kyra when he recounts how his action might be perceived by people with evil minds (94). He is also open enough to examine his attraction to Mattie and the difference in their ages. In fact he resists her movement toward a physical relationship because he is concerned both about the custody case and about his own motives. The kind of self-reflection Mike exhibits is an indication of a deeper analysis of the emergence of sensitive male characters—characters whose emotional responses match those of females. Men's studies looks to these portrayals as an indication of society's ability to accommodate all types of male characters.

However, the elevation of men into roles usually held by women, such as sensitive partner or caring parent, can also lead to the erasure of women's roles in a work. While King's characterization of Mike presents an excellent example of the changing depiction of men in fiction, a feminist analysis might question why the increase in Mike's role is accomplished at the expense of lessening the importance of women in the novel. All of the important female characters are either dead (Mattie, Johanna) or dead and crazy (Rogette, Sara) at its end. And all of these women either were or wanted to be mothers. These different approaches to the novel are examples of the ways that various critical approaches may focus on certain points and read them in opposing manners. But both approaches would agree that the character of Mike represents a sensitive analysis of depth possible in the creation of a male fictional character.

7

Hearts in Atlantis
(1999)

While Stephen King has always carefully constructed his works, *Hearts in Atlantis* continues a more recent trend toward the integration of complex form and content in his fiction. This book is not a single novel but rather a collection of interrelated stories; two are novella length, two are short stories, and the book closes with what might be seen as an epilogue. *Hearts in Atlantis* may be composed of five different stories, but it is obvious that the book is meant to be read sequentially like a novel. The parts are introduced by similar title pages and their unity is underlined by the lack of a table of contents. Each section is connected to a specific year, epigraph, and title: "1960: They had a stick sharpened at both ends/Low Men in Yellow Coats"; "1966: Man, we just couldn't stop laughing/Hearts in Atlantis"; "1983: Gobless us every one/Blind Willie"; "1999: When someone dies, you think about the past/Why We're in Vietnam"; and "1999: Come on, you bastard, come on home/Heavenly Shades of Night Are Falling." The dates mark the passing of time. The epigraphs suggest an important element in each story, and the titles summarize one aspect of their contents. The complex organization of the book is mirrored by its treatment of its central theme. In *Hearts in Atlantis*, King directly confronts the effect of U.S. involvement in Vietnam upon those who fought and those who remained at home.

Three more epigraphs appear before the first story and serve as an introduction to the work as a whole by suggesting the breadth of King's concerns. The first epigraph is an exchange from the television show *The Prisoner*, about getting information; this enigmatic show dealt with a man who is held in an unknown place for an unknown reason. The second epigraph is a quotation from William Golding's *Lord of the Flies*, a novel about boys stranded on an island that figures in the first novella in *Hearts in Atlantis*. The citation deals specifically with Simon's perception of the image of a dead sow and its connection to adult views of the world. The third epigraph is from the film *Easy Rider*. "We blew it" indicates not only a summation of the film but also an accurate reflection of the attitude held by many members of the generation who found this story of the death of hope for the youth movement of the 1960s reflected in their own lives.

These epigraphs and the title of the book also illustrate King's ongoing use of elements of popular culture to develop his ideas. While "Hearts" reverberates thematically in many aspects of the novel, "Atlantis" refers to a popular song of that era by Donovan that deals with the lost continent and the idyllic past it represents. "Heavenly Shades of Night Are Falling" is a phrase from yet another song, this one by a popular group known as The Platters. The title of the song, "Twilight Time," refers to the time of day when it is played and also to the theme of the passage of time that permeates the work. The epigraphs that open the book and the titles and statements that open each segment cover a range of elements in popular culture from literature and music to television and film. They all combine to unite theme and structure in this complex work.

PLOT DEVELOPMENT

In *Hearts in Atlantis*, King interweaves events and characters to construct a text in which five separate stories are ultimately conjoined. Each story has its own internal organization distinguishing it from the others. The point of view shifts in each of the stories from an omniscient narrative to a limited third-person to first-person narrative. The first section is divided into chapters with descriptions of the events to follow; the second section only has chapter numbers; the third section is divided by times of day; and the last two sections have no divisions at all. While the length of each story decreases, the time elapsed between each section increases. But King manages to connect them by introducing characters and events that are shared by all.

"Low Men in Yellow Coats"

King opens the book by connecting events in *Hearts in Atlantis* to his earlier works of fiction by joining fantasy to the reality that permeates this book. The title ultimately reveals the relationship between the realm of this story and that of such novels as *Insomnia* and the Dark Tower series where King's worldview is developed. His characters in those novels are involved in an heroic quest to reach the tower by following the path of the beam. In *Hearts in Atlantis* one of the characters has a dream of the tower as "a still spindle upon which all of existence moved and spun" (165). But the book also presents another instance of King's interest in the moment of transition between childhood and adulthood. Bobby Garfield recalls the events of the summer of 1960 in Harwich, Connecticut, and its surrounding area. The narrative moves back and forth between the boy's childhood experiences and his adult understanding of this crucial period. The fantasy world of childhood is connected to King's universe of the Dark Tower in its use of the perspective of time. For Bobby, the further he gets from the events of that summer, the less real it seems—like all childhood fantasy.

The opening scene, which takes place on Bobby Garfield's eleventh birthday, introduces the plot. Bobby's widowed mother is such a miser that, instead of buying him the bicycle he wants, she gives something that heralds his passage into adulthood: an adult library card. Embittered by the untimely death of her husband, Randall, a real estate salesman, Liz Garfield works as a secretary for his former boss. While the story is told from Bobby's perspective, a limited, third-person point of view, the reader soon gains an understanding of the mother-child relationship. Bobby reminds Liz of her husband, whom she viewed as a gambling loser. She fears Bobby will follow his example.

Bobby may be too innocent to interpret the long hours his mother spends with the boss as anything but job-related until he is shocked by an incident that occurs at the end of the story. But the reader can sense her frustration, her thwarted ambition, and the limitations imposed by the opposite sex that force her to use physical attraction to hold her job. King adds another element into this troubled family situation with the arrival of a new boarder in the apartment house where they live.

Ted Brautigan emerges from a taxi just as Liz leaves for work and Bobby departs for school. Liz's negative attitude toward Ted is influenced by his use of shopping bags as part of his luggage; she is unable, for much of the story, to get his name right and insists on calling him

"Mr. Brattigan." While Bobby senses his mother's disapproval of his relationship with Ted, this man fascinates him. King effectively captures the world of a child who must find ways to do what he thinks is right within the limitations imposed by adults who do not understand. Ted will be just as instrumental as Bobby's mother in educating the boy and enabling him to grow up, but both will mark him in ways that haunt him for the rest of his life. The last element in Bobby's growth and development is the introduction of his two friends, characters who move in and out of the other stories in *Hearts in Atlantis*: Carol Gerber and John Sullivan (known as Sully-John). The interaction between these characters generates three plot lines.

The dominant plot refers to the title of the story—the low men in yellow coats. Learning of Bobby's desire for a bicycle, Ted hires him for a variety of jobs. As an excuse generated to hide his true actions from his mother, Bobby is to "read the newspaper" for Ted. In actuality, Ted wants Bobby to check the neighborhood for certain signs of the appearance of low men in yellow coats. The men are low in the sense that they are dangerous and crude. Signs of their presence that Bobby should report are: false lost pet posters, upside-down, hand-printed for sale notices, the town clock ringing at the wrong time, kite tails caught hanging, and stars and crescent moons on hopscotch grids.

The two secondary plots deal with injuries received by the two women in the story. All three plots unite when Liz decides to go to a seminar with her boss and two male co-workers. When all other alternatives are exhausted, she agrees to let Ted sit for Bobby. While she is gone, Ted takes Bobby to see the movie *Village of the Damned* in the nearby town of Bridgeport. The adult Bobby recalls this film as the last movie of his childhood. They walk to a bar in a strange, run-down part of the city. Ted places a bet at The Corner Pocket Pool and Billiards, where Bobby meets a woman who remembers his father and has a different perception of this man than his mother does. For this woman Randall was a nice, generous, funny guy, not the gambling addict that Liz remembers. The separation from his mother's perspective that is part of the transition to the adult world is increased by this knowledge. In a cab on their way home they pass a car that fits Ted's description of the flashy, vulgar vehicles of the low men. When they get home Ted explains that these men come from another world. Ted has sensed their presence and has placed a bet to get enough money to escape.

Terrible events happen in the chapter titled "Ugly Thursday," the day Liz is scheduled to return. Bobby goes for a walk and hears Carol crying for him. He drops his Alvin Dark baseball glove when he finds her. The boys that threatened them earlier have now beaten her. One of them, Willie Shearman, appears in other stories in this book. When Carol faints from the pain they've inflicted, Bobby somehow finds the strength to carry her to his house. Ted manages to fix her dislocated shoulder, but just as he is wiping off her cheeks Liz returns early because she has been sexually attacked by the men at the seminar. In Liz's suspicious, sexually oriented viewpoint, it appears that Ted has molested Carol, just as Liz has feared he might assault her own son. Her reaction to her own situation (of which we are not yet aware) leads her to attack both Ted and Bobby. At that moment men are the source of all evil.

Because Ted has touched Carol, she gains temporary powers that allow her to see and describe Liz's attack and rape by her boss and co-workers. According to Ted, Liz is a foolish woman who should have known what was going to happen when she went with the men. He feels that she let her greed overrule her common sense. Ted agrees to leave in order to placate Liz. When Bobby and Ted embrace, Bobby is also left with a vision of what went on between his mother and her boss, and how she hadn't really understood fully what could happen.

When Bobby discovers one of the posters offering a reward for information about a lost dog named Brautigan in his mother's room, he believes that she has sold information about Ted to the low men for money. Bobby returns to The Corner Pocket, where Ted will come to claim his bet, but he cannot save his friend. The low men have trapped them both. Ted agrees to go with them but insists that Bobby remain behind. Ted is identified as a "breaker." In exchange for Bobby's freedom, he will do his job willingly. The low men want Bobby to decide. Bobby fails the test and opts to stay with his mother rather than sacrifice himself for Ted. He senses his choice is unheroic, but he is not brave enough to face the low men. Bobby returns to the bar and gets a ride home and the money Ted had won. He gives the money to his mother. The image of Liz's face as she sees Ted's money never leaves Bobby: "Yet some new and not particularly pleasant part of him enjoyed that look—how it rendered her old and ugly and comic, a person who was stupid as well as avaricious" (232).

These events change Bobby. He can no longer act like a hero. He avenges Carol's beating but continues to get into trouble with the police. One day he gets a letter from Carol that contains an envelope filled with dark red rose petals, a message from Ted. Bobby's final legacy from Ted is the understanding that Ted is free again in one of the parallel worlds that exist connected to the tower. Bobby realizes he must carry on. If he cannot be a hero he must just do the best he can.

"Hearts in Atlantis"

This novella is written as a first-person narrative and is set in a short period of time during 1966. It relates events in the lives of several students at the University of Maine and is, perhaps, a reflection of King's own experience during the Vietnam War. High blood pressure, ruptured eardrums, and flat feet kept him out of the conflict and enabled him to stay in college. The story is a break from the fantasy elements that permeate the end of "Low Men" and marks a shift for King in its avoidance of the supernatural. The narrator, Peter Riley, is a freshman who tells the story to record an example of the intensity of the changes facing students toward the end of the 1960s. This story continues the movement between past and present that marked the first story of the book. While Pete learned a great deal during college, the first major lesson marking his transition to adulthood is related to with the card game known as Hearts.

The game of Hearts takes over the third floor of Chamberlain, Pete's dormitory, and becomes an addiction few can resist. Most of the young men on this floor must maintain a 2.5 average to stay in school because their studies are funded by scholarships and loans. The central conflict in this story is between the need to maintain a C average and stay out of the draft for the Vietnam War and the lure of the ongoing game of Hearts that threatens failure.

Chief among those playing Hearts is Ronnie Malenfant, who will also appear in other stories in *Hearts in Atlantis*. Pete's roommate, Nate Hoppenstand, and the outsider who walks with the aid of crutches, Stokely Jones III, are among those who resist the game. While Nate tries to avoid any involvement with the antiwar movement, Stokely, dubbed Rip-Rip by Ronnie because of the sound he makes as he moves, becomes an activist. Stokely introduces the peace sign to the dorm. Pete is drawn into the game, but he is also interested in the protest movement, especially since Carol Gerber, whom he dates, is involved.

Carol dated Sully-John in the first story, and she remembers Bobby as she shows Pete a photo of the three of them (Carol, Sully-John, and Bobby) when they were young and tells him about the day she was hurt. Bobby is wearing his baseball glove, and she now knows that Willie Shearman took it from the park. The past constantly affects the present. Carol marches in an antiwar protest because Bobby did what was right on that day in 1960.

This story also demonstrates the connection among the various narratives in *Hearts in Atlantis*. While characters seem to make independent decisions, every choice and action reverberates throughout the book. While "Low Men" connects the world of the narrative to the rest of King's fiction, this story links characters in the book to each other and further demonstrates the effect of the past on the present. Pete's relationship with Carol is one of the events that ultimately save him from the game and Vietnam. She encourages him to quit Hearts, and even though she must leave to care for her mother, she does inspire him to study for a while. But his ultimate salvation comes from the person who is least involved with the rest of the dorm—Stokely.

As was the case in the first story, a major event changes a character's life—even if she or he is not central to the story. Pete has been drawn back into the game and plays the night of a big storm on campus. The next day students find an antiwar symbol spray-painted on the wall of the dorm. Later that day, rain turns the snow to slush. The cardplayers look out the window to see Stokely moving so fast on his crutches that he finally slips and falls down. While they can't resist laughing hysterically at the image he creates, Pete attempts to stop when he remembers Carol told him that her attack began with the boys' joking; suddenly it was no longer a joke. Pete and the others rush out to help Stokely. Their carrying Stokely recalls Bobby's rescue of Carol, although this time the participants are less heroic because they have been laughing at the victim. This event finally leads Pete to quit the game.

At a dorm meeting that night the dean accuses Stokely of painting the graffiti because he is the only one who wears a peace symbol. Others in the dorm gradually reveal how they have been adopting the symbol themselves. The previously uncommitted Nate explains its invention by the philosopher Bertrand Russell, who based it on British semaphore signs to stand for nuclear disarmament. Since there is no proof that Stokely actually did the graffiti, he is not blamed for it. He is not happy, however, because he wants to take responsibility for his protest. He goes on to become an activist lawyer. Carol, too, becomes an activist. For much of the book it appears that she has died in a Weather Underground-like explosion. (The Weather Underground was a notorious radical protest group of the period.)

These two characters choose heroic activity and sacrifice just like Ted Brautigan. Pete receives clippings about Carol's protest activities that Christmas. She also sends him a copy of the book that had been so important for Bobby, *Lord of the Flies*. Rather than an inscription, the title page contains the images of a heart plus a peace sign equaling information. Pete also gets involved in the protest movement and lands in a holding cell during the Democratic convention in Chicago, but he resembles Bobby in not choosing a more central role. The story ends with an incident long after the main events—a reunion between Pete and one of his college friends. No matter what happened, they both agree that they tried during that period. They were not the big heroes, but they did something—just as Bobby saved Carol but failed with Ted. King suggests that any positive action is important even if it is not truly heroic.

"Blind Willie"

This story takes place in a single day, a much shorter time span than the previous two works, but it also moves back and forth in time. King uses the details of one day in the life of one character to reflect on the ways in which the past controls the present. "Blind Willie" is also more directly concerned with the effects of Vietnam than the first two narratives. The title character is Willie Shearman, the boy who betrayed and joined in beating Carol in "Low Men." Even though he saved Sully-John's life in Vietnam, Willie spends the rest of his life atoning for both real and imagined harm he has done to others. The defining moment in his life was the attack on Carol, when he was not heroic enough to challenge his friends. Even his courageous actions in the war are not redemptive. Instead, he has devised a daily plan; a life's work that allows him to stand in for all of those who watch while evil is done. King details the daily transformation of Bill Shearman into Blind Willie, the Vietnam veteran who begs for a living. While giving the reader this view of one man's life, he uses the extreme realism of the details he presents to cross over into a world beyond realism: a world where all of the actions seem true even though the resulting effect is fantasy.

Integral to the impression of realism in "Blind Willie" is the story's organization. Each stage in the day is marked by a specific time. Bill's alarm goes off at 6:15 in the morning. At first, it seems that he is just another businessman off to the city for a day at the office as he puts on his suit and tie. His wife reminds him to bring home eggnog for guests they are having over that night. A reference to Atlantis during his train ride briefly connects this story to others in book. On the way to his office at 8:40 he gives a beggar some change, defending his action to a passerby through a reference to the Christmas season. The "gobless you" he receives in response from the man is the source of the epigraph for this story. Even though his wife's name is Sharon, she is transformed into Carol in a discussion on the elevator. Vietnam makes its first appearance in this story because the man reminds him of a soldier returning from Tam Boi in the A Shau Valley.

Once Bill enters his fifth-floor office behind the door labeled WEST-ERN STATES LAND ANALYSTS, the transformation begins. He climbs through the ceiling into another office on the sixth floor. Vietnam pho-tographs and a copy of his honorable discharge, which was awarded the day he saved Sully-John, decorate the wall of the character that is now called Willie. When Willie undresses and carefully hangs his clothing in a closet, the accumulation of details indicates a world hidden behind the businessman's facade. Willie puts on simple workingman clothing and dog tags. He then begins his penance by writing, "I am heartily sorry" (421) over and over again in a ledger. He then puts on his highly pol-ished jump boots and further changes his appearance through the ap-plication of makeup and hair gel. But his transformation and acts of penance are not complete.

At 10:00 in the Whitmore Hotel he changes from Willie Shearman to Blind Willie Garfield, the Vietnam veteran. As with the other alterations, small details such as dark glasses and a cane modify his appearance. The irony is that at a certain point, the disguise becomes reality as he loses and then regains his ability to see during the day. His current temporary blindness is connected to his lack of vision during his rescue of Sullivan. Just as Bobby, whose last name he has adopted, was able to find the strength to carry Carol on the day she was attacked, so Willie was able to carry a body heavier than his own on the day Sullivan was shot. He leaves the hotel and by 10:15 takes up his position in front of St. Patrick's Cathedral. His sign identifies him as former Lt. William J. Garfield and recounts where he lost his vision in Vietnam. He further develops his problems by indicating he has lost his benefits and his home. He uses an old baseball glove, the one he stole from Bobby, to hold the money people give him. While he is very successful at this job, it is not easy. King describes in great detail the precise position he must maintain, which is very similar to the military parade rest that projects pride tem-pered by humility. Again the careful details of the description mask the impossibility of anyone actually living this way.

The pattern of Willie's day is altered only by Officer Wheelock, who thinks he knows the truth about Willie's deception and comes to get his share of the take. While the officer waits, Willie discusses the A Shau Valley with another vet, mentioning Lieutenant Dieffenbaker, who will appear in the next story in the book. Wheelock thinks conversations like this one will make Willie reveal his deception, but Willie knows the world is complicated and that what seems false may actually be true.

The payoff to Wheelock is the most dangerous moment of the day because the policeman is not happy with his current take and wants more. Willie is afraid the officer will follow him and his careful routine will be destroyed. At 4:25 he begins to reverse the process that began the day. He uses a different hotel during his transformation, but otherwise the details remain the same.

While these details provide the framework for the story, Willie's thoughts provide the background that makes his world understandable. Not only does he discuss his experiences in Vietnam with those who give him money, but the also constantly returns to Bobby and Bobby's actions in the past. He once again writes in his ledger of his regret for hurting Carol. In addition to his memories, he has a scrapbook that marks the past that includes a long section detailing Carol's life, the bomb that goes off at the wrong time and kills six, and her possible death. A newspaper clipping describes Carol's attempt to retrieve the defective device. All of these actions bring a kind of peace to Willie, who resumes his identity as Bill Shearman and returns home with the eggnog.

The story comes full circle. It is midnight and Bill is in bed with his wife. They discuss his work, his decision to take a little time off, his search for a new location, and their guests. The realistic details that transformed Bill into a fantastic Blind Willie now return him to the ordinary world of husbands and wives in bed. In his dreams Bill goes back to his work and then even that fades. The alarm goes off and a new day begins.

"Why We're in Vietnam"

This story takes place in an even shorter period of time than the last one, but like "Blind Willie" it moves from realism to fantasy smoothly. "Why We're in Vietnam" continues the pattern of integrating the past and present. In the opening sentence, Sully acknowledges how a death brings the past to one's mind. This story takes place on the day of the funeral of one of the men he was with in Vietnam, twenty-six years after the United States evacuated Saigon.

Sully recalls the day when he was injured and Willie Shearman saved him. But that day also marked the first appearance of the *mamasan*, a specter of an old Vietnamese woman, whom he alone can see. Doctors managed to replace his intestines and repair one of his testicles, injuries he received in Vietnam, but nothing can remove the apparition. His other thoughts are similar to those of Willie—reflections about Carol and her antiwar activities. The old Vietnamese woman is never far away. He knows she was initially associated with Ronnie Malenfant and an incident in a village, but now she haunts Sully.

The opening of the story details Sully's relationship with the *mamasan*: those points in his life when she haunts him and his attempts to free himself from her. Psychiatry does not help. He knows that in reality she is not there, but he still can see her. He understands she is a result of his experiences in Vietnam, and her presence helps him cope with his memories. His past is set against the details of his trip to the funeral in New York City. He now runs a car dealership in Milford, a city twenty miles from his childhood home in Harwich. Dick Pagano, the dead man, was involved in all of the events that haunt Sully when he thinks of Vietnam.

Gradually, during the course of the funeral and Sully's drive home, King reveals the episodes that marked the day thirty years ago that changed so many lives in the war. First there was a helicopter crash; those who tried to rescue the victims are caught in enemy fire. Sully tripped a mine that caused more enemy fire. When they enter a village, Malenfant sticks his bayonet into the old woman. Lieutenant Dieffenbaker signals to one of his men to shoot Malenfant's buddy before the attack turns into another My Lai massacre. The *mamasan* is in Sully's car as he gets caught in traffic, and he replays his conversation with Dieffenbaker outside after the funeral about the legacies of Vietnam such as cancer, failed marriages, and addictions.

His memories turn into fantasy as he sees a wide range of consumer products, from microwave ovens to popular magazines, fall out of the sky onto the people stuck in the traffic jam. Sully sees the falling objects as the incoming fire from Vietnam. And he returns to his conversation with Dieffenbaker that eventually turns to the difference between memory and the images in one's mind. The lieutenant confesses that Malenfant is his version of the *mamasan*, a person who haunts his life. None of them have ever really escaped from Vietnam; the experiences they endured obsess them. But their actions did not change the world.

The possessions their generation enjoys are markers of the fact that nothing has really changed. The falling objects are symbols of the betrayal of the hopes of his generation for Sully. Bobby's baseball glove brings him back to the summer of 1960. Sully walks back toward the *mamasan* and feels safe in her embrace. When Dieffenbaker reads of the episode in the paper the next day, the reader learns that Sully died of a heart attack in the traffic jam. Dieffenbaker realizes that Sully's death is yet another indication of the fact that the war ends a little at a time for each individual.

"Heavenly Shades of Night Are Falling"

This story is an epilogue to the rest of the narratives in *Hearts in Atlantis*. King returns to the first location mentioned in the book, Harwich, and to an afternoon and evening in the life of Bobby. He, too, recalls the past as he attends the memorial service for Sully. Much has changed since he left the town, and all appears normal. There is no evidence of the low men in the hopscotch grid he passes. He visits the old apartment building and makes his last stop the place where he found Carol on the day of the beating. He takes a radio from his gym bag as he thinks of Sully. A woman speaks to him, and he recognizes Carol, who he thought was dead. She has changed her name and identity. They share events from their past and their current lives. Bobby tells her how he received the baseball glove from Sully-John's executor.

He feels Ted is involved in its return because the address he finds includes "Zone 11" (520), an address that doesn't exist. Carol knows Willie took it, but they can't understand how it got to Sully-John. Bobby believes Ted sent it to inform him of Sully's death and Carol's existence. In addition to the address there is another piece of paper, the title page from a copy of *Lord of the Flies*. A message written on the page indicates that Bobby should tell Carol *"she was as brave as a lion"* (521). There is also another message for Carol, the symbol of a heart plus a peace sign equaling information.

Bobby replaces the glove under the tree, where he left it so many years ago. Even though things have come full circle, both of them know they cannot recapture the past. They can only attempt to understand what has happened and remember the events and people who were important to them. At the end of the story The Platters begin to sing the words that make up the title of this story.

CHARACTER DEVELOPMENT

There are many characters in *Hearts in Atlantis*, but only a few appear in more than one story. These characters, along with the events they experience, unify the stories in a way that is more than just the sum of their parts. The passage of time that is central to this work also affects the development of their personalities. King is able to trace the ways that people change over time and the ways that events in the past are viewed in the present. One overriding concern is the focus on all of the characters and the manner in which they operate in moments of deep stress. As in *Dreamcatcher* King uses their reactions to crisis to examine the nature of heroism in modern America.

Often these stressful events coincide with or precipitate transformations from one stage in a character's development to another, like the passage from childhood to adulthood. At the end of the book, King deals with the ultimate transition to death, where past and present become one because there is no future. The principal characters in *Hearts in Atlantis* all develop in the course of the book. They respond to the events of their childhood and youth by adapting to the challenges they encounter. Their responses mark them forever, and they may spend the rest of their lives dealing with these defining moments. The ongoing battle in King's fantastic universe to follow the beam and keep the world from falling apart is mirrored by later actions in the real world. In all cases a character is tested in a way that usually involves both an individual's integrity and his or her loyalty to the group.

Bobby Garfield

Bobby Garfield's actions form the core of the book. While he may not physically appear in each of the stories, the events of his eleventh summer permeate the book. His experiences are balanced against the later encounters of other characters with the war in Vietnam. Bobby faces two tests. He passes one and fails the other. Both his success and his failure come from the traits that make up his personality and those things he learns over the course of that summer.

Bobby resembles many of the young boys who appear as characters in King's work such as Mark Petrie in *'Salem's Lot*, but in "Low Men in Yellow Coats" both King and his character look back on the events of 1960 in hindsight. While some of the events Bobby must face are fantastic, his response is more realistic than it might have been in King's earlier fiction. Bobby does the best he can in the face of circumstances, but he can only do so much. He can find the strength to save Carol, but he cannot sacrifice himself to save Ted. The world of the men in yellow coats is too terrifying for him to take the heroic course of action.

King introduces the novel *Lord of the Flies* to explain how children have a limited ability to cope with the difficult challenges of the adult world. In William Golding's novel, a group of children stranded on an island become savages, unable to maintain the façade of civilization. The novel ends with their rescue by adults and the final question that puzzles

Bobby about who will save the adults. The novel's analysis of the nature of heroism is reflected in *Hearts in Atlantis*.

Even though the book presents multiple levels of awareness for the characters because of the continuous passage between past and present, Bobby is not aware of the effect of his actions on others. He lives with the knowledge that he did the best he could at the time but failed the test of true heroism. He has come to terms with his actions by first striking out against society and getting in trouble after the incidents in Harwich. But by the end of the book he has settled down to life as a father and husband supporting his family by working as a carpenter. For Bobby and Carol the fact that they come back to Harwich and the site of tragedy and heroism is proof that not all of the magic of childhood is gone. Bobby's memories of the men in yellow coats may have dimmed, but he still believes in Ted, who somehow knew that Carol would join him in a final farewell to childhood.

Carol Gerber

One of a trio of childhood friends in "Low Men in Yellow Coats," Carol Gerber is a part of most of the narratives in *Hearts in Atlantis*. She is Bobby Garfield's first love and the occasion of his defining act of heroism when he carries her home after she has been beaten. But she and Pete Riley share a first sexual encounter in "Hearts in Atlantis," and her later life is a reference point for Sully at the moment of his death. She is also the focus of Willie Shearman's acts of atonement in "Blind Willie." By the end of the book she has transformed herself into the new identity of Denise Schoonover who teaches at Vassar. Of all of the characters, Carol goes through the most radical changes in the course of her life.

She is introduced as Bobby's first love, the girl who kisses him on the cheek and gives him a birthday card. In "Hearts in Atlantis," Carol, who has been dating Sully-John, forms a relationship with her classmate, Pete Riley. She also begins the radical war protest activity that will shape her life. Her decisions are directed by her experience with Bobby. She chooses to actively protest the war because Bobby stood up for her, and this action was the most important thing that anyone did for her in her life. Carol goes on to join an underground group. She is unable to prevent a bomb explosion that kills several people and is later believed to have died when a house explodes in Los Angeles.

Even though she changes her identity, her basic belief system remains intact throughout her life. Bobby realizes that Carol can see the true character of people because of her strong observational powers. She is the only one he trusts with information about the low men, and she believes him. Pete, too, recognizes her insight about people. While Willie does not really know her, he spends his life attempting to live up to the standards Bobby set with her.

At the end she has forgotten some things and has changed some of her traits; for example, she once hated math, but Denise now teaches it. But she still recognizes the importance of the old message about the heart and the peace sign equaling information. She leaves the university to take care of her mother, but she sends Pete that message at Christmas on the title page of a copy of *Lord of the Flies*—the title page that reappears at the end of the novel. Her life may change, but the symbols that guide it remain the same.

John Sullivan

John Sullivan, also known as Sully-John or Sully in the different stories, is the focus of "Why We're in Vietnam." Sully is another example of a person who finds the strength to act heroically for a few moments when faced with a crisis, but he also wonders about his courage in other situations. He never really knows why he acted as he did and sees himself as an ordinary guy caught in extraordinary circumstances.

In "Low Men in Yellow Coats," Sully is not present when Carol is attacked or when Bobby must decide about following Ted. He is a good friend, but he is not challenged by the events in the story; the same is true in "Hearts in Atlantis," where he is the boy back home who is dating Carol and waiting to go to Vietnam. Even though he is not the central character in "Blind Willie," he is important. Willie's one moment of redemption comes in saving Sully's life. Sully reviews his activities in Vietnam on the last day of his life in "Why We're in Vietnam."

He won the Silver Star for rescuing one of the men in a helicopter crash, and that is the first action on the day when he gets shot and when he sees the old woman killed. Sully has become a car dealer who suffers from some of the problems facing veterans. In the story he reflects on the distance between the events in Vietnam and his present concerns and how time alters perceptions. He is still haunted by a vision of the old woman Malenfant killed. Although he never really expresses it, his return to that moment raises questions. The lieutenant was able to signal the order for one of his men to kill another in order to stop the massacre, but Sully never knows what he would have done if the lieutenant had not acted. This question is the reason he is still haunted by the dead woman. His last image is of Bobby's glove, an object from another time where he did not act because he did not have the opportunity. He dies never having been really tested.

William Shearman

Because he failed the first time he was challenged, William Shearman, also known as Bill and Blind Willie, spends the rest of his life trying to atone for his actions. Willie was afraid to protest when Carol was beaten. He doesn't know if he would have been able to stop Harry Doolin if Harry hadn't stopped after he dislocated her shoulder. His life was changed when he was unable to become a hero. Nothing he does in Vietnam helps him get over his earlier failure.

His story is the most unique in the book. He has chosen to live his entire life in the shadow of his youthful mistake. In the past Willie appeared to go along with the other boys; now he challenges the relationship between appearance and reality. To the policeman he appears to impersonate a veteran to make money, but Willie actually becomes that veteran and even loses his sight for part of the day. While he does assume another persona, it is not that far from the reality of his experience in Vietnam. He becomes heroic in the way he chooses to atone for his lack of heroism in the past.

THEME

The effect of the past on the present, transitional moments in life, the relationship between appearance and reality, the effect of history on the individual, and the connection between the individual and the group are all themes that are amplified in *Hearts in Atlantis* under an overriding concern for the nature of the hero. Each of the five stories with their interconnecting plots and characters examines various aspects of these ideas. The themes also serve to unite the events in the stories that define the characters' lives. Much of what happens in the book is set against the war in Vietnam. All other important moments refer to the war and its effect on American society. Vietnam places the other episodes in the story in a different perspective than they might have in another King work that does not focus on it. In a collision between reality and fantasy, traditional views of the heroic are no longer valid. All of the other themes contribute to King's examination of this idea. In most of his genre fiction a hero emerges to save society. The Vietnam War caused people to question just how to act under pressure and what they might do in certain situations. Simple views of the heroic were no longer possible for many.

In "Low Men in Yellow Coats," King's fantasy world is set against a society that is just beginning to learn about Vietnam. One of the newspapers Bobby reads to Ted deals with the intensification of skirmishes in that country. That war will later touch Bobby's world, but the universe Ted inhabits runs parallel to it, only breaking into our world on rare occasions. Those moments of contact give rise to Bobby's understanding of the nature of heroism and reality. When Ted gives Bobby a copy of *Lord of the Flies*, Bobby first encounters ideas about mob mentality and the role of the individual. This book, along with the film *Village of the Damned* (about children with special powers), provides examples of both group dynamics and the role of heroes and adults. Only one adult can deal with the children in this film, and he sacrifices himself to destroy them since they cannot be taught how to incorporate morality with their ability to control others.

Bobby considers this film the last great film of his childhood. After seeing it he begins to understand the troubled roles adults must play in their own lives and those of others. He also has a vision of the nature of heroism, as this is his first experience with a hero who does not survive. When Bobby carries Carol home, he acts as the traditional hero, but when he chooses to allow Ted to sacrifice himself rather than go with him, King unites many of his themes. Bobby sees the difference between adult and childhood choices. Heroism is not a simple option. His mother's greedy betrayal of Ted becomes an example of bad choices made by an individual. He also learns how to see beneath the surface of things, questioning reality. Do the men in yellow coats exist, who can see them, and why? "Low Men in Yellow Coats" raises these questions in the context of childhood, even though it is childhood filtered through time and memory. In the next story, King further develops these themes with college students.

"Hearts in Atlantis" places the questions raised by the first story into another context. While continuing the pattern of opposing events that take place in the past with later perceptions of them, this narrative uses "hearts" as a metaphor for its thematic explorations. In Vietnam, the goal was to capture the hearts and minds of the Vietnamese. Hearts is the game that consumes the narrator and his classmates, and the description of the game resembles that of a war. In both cases a mob mentality can lead to disaster: either the destruction of careers in school or the slaughter of villagers. Ronnie Malenfant participates in both actions as he is an avid cardplayer at school and later kills the old woman in Vietnam and almost precipitates a massacre. But the metaphoric use of the word also suggests the dual idea of heart as courage and the heart involved in a love relationship.

The key message that ends both this chapter and the book uses the drawing of a heart with an arrow through it along with the peace symbol to equal information. The game of Hearts is an escape from the real world of classes and school, but those who continue to play will go to an even more real world, that of Vietnam. The lure of the game is an addiction that only a few can resist, ironically among those who resist are those not threatened by the draft—Carol, a woman, and Stokely, who is handicapped. But even these two characters do not escape the need to make choices about how to operate in the face of the war. They become most involved in the protest against the war, and their choices reverberate throughout the story. Because of their actions Pete also opts for heroism by rescuing Stokely, a deed that frees him from his obsession with the game of Hearts, just as his love for Carol provides his first break with the game.

In "Blind Willie," King goes to the heart of the questions about heroism generated by the events in the stories. The idea of heroic action is tied to that of appearance. Sometimes, as he suggests, things are not as they seem. Willie sees Bobby as a successful hero, but Bobby knows of his own failure to act. The world sees Willie as the winner of the Silver Star or as the blind veteran who begs to survive. All of these perceptions contain some truth. But there is a gap between the characters' self-evaluation and that of the world. At times, as King suggests, heroism is not so much the result of choice as it is of luck, of being in the right place at the right time and acting without thinking. It is the heart and not the mind that can define a person's life.

When Willie reflects on his actions and on Carol's, he is really questioning the definition of hero. He views Carol's participation in the bombing as his fault, and he feels responsible for the deaths of the people in the attack. His inability to react against the pull of the mob in her beating has changed the course of their personal histories, and the effects have spread to lives beyond their own. While it may be difficult to identify or define heroism, its absence creates a class of people who see themselves as failures because they do not measure up to society's ideals. But perhaps "Blind Willie" and the other stories suggest that the heroic image is a product of the same popular culture that dominates life in the

United States. In the real world, there are no Supermen—only ordinary people doing the best they can to cope with events that are too much for them to handle.

Consumer images dominate the story ironically titled "Why We're in Vietnam." Sully dies amid a barrage of products falling from the sky. His memories of terrible events during the war are played against his thoughts about the new demo that he drives, the route he takes to the funeral and home, his auto dealership, and how veterans can be identified by the Zippo lighters they use. Even the dead man's illness, pancreatic cancer, is associated with a star—Michael Landon. As he vividly recalls the events of the day when he acted heroically, witnessed Malenfant's killing of the villager, and his own near-death injury, he compares the burned men from the helicopter crash to TV dinners. The images of aging veterans with big bellies and thinning hair contradict the usual views of heroes.

Just as the men who were buddies during the war really have little in common anymore, so the impact of their actions fades. The truth lives in the memories of those who survive. Now they are not capable of heroism; the events in their lives no longer provide the occasion for it. Like Sully and his *mamasan*, the survivors are haunted by the ghosts of having one soldier kill another and can only talk angrily about the effects of the past. Sully lives with the same question as Willie—Would he have done anything to stop Malenfant from killing the Vietnamese woman?—just as Willie questions his role in Carol's beating. While Willie spends the rest of his life atoning for his lack of heroism, Sully buries himself in consumerism but cannot rid himself of his ghost.

Carol and Bobby honor the ghosts in their lives in "Heavenly Shades of Night Are Falling." The book comes full circle in this story, where the participants revisit the past. Bobby places the baseball glove, which has figured in many lives, back where he left it so long ago. He and Carol know they cannot recapture the past; they can only attempt to understand it. Ted may have escaped again, lives go on in the face of death, identities are altered, but the past cannot be forgotten. Some of the magic of childhood remains in the adults. Perhaps they survive because they still retain the memories of their childhood beliefs. The talismans of their youth, the books and images of their past, still have meaning. They can return to the past and still distinguish it from the present. They know the difference between fictional heroes and people who must live in the real world. Even the old songs are still important. They have achieved a kind of peace reflected in the song whose words provide its title, "Heavenly Shades of Night Are Falling."

ALTERNATIVE READING: VIETNAM NARRATIVES

Vietnam literature can be considered a specific genre. It encompasses all types of fiction and can cross other genre lines. There can be mystery or horror novels that are also considered Vietnam fiction. Of course the most important element in defining this literature is that the work deals directly with the involvement of the United States in Vietnam. Because the United States gradually became more and more involved with Southeast Asia, Graham Greene's novel *The Quiet American*, published in 1955 (one year after the fall of the French fortress at Dien Bien Phu signaled that country's military retreat from Indochina), is considered to be the first novel in this genre.

While the war officially ended with the peace agreement signing in 1973, Vietnam novels continue to appear. The genre includes works that cover a wide range of concepts. This fiction can present the soldier's life in Vietnam, events in the United States during the war, and the after-effects of the war in this country. In addition to dealing with the war, the fiction generally features personal narratives that focus on the American experience where the Vietnamese are secondary characters.

Hearts in Atlantis certainly qualifies as a work of the Vietnam literature genre. By looking at the book in the context of this genre, another view of it becomes evident. Vietnam and American involvement with this country unite the narratives. The five stories cover a range of reactions to the war both at home and in the field. The time span allows King to trace the effects of the war from its early stages to its later effects on the veterans. The different personal narratives allow him to examine a variety of attitudes toward it. By placing the war in the forefront of this book, King shifts the focus of his fiction from horror to a genre that can be associated with major, serious works of literature.

King sets the first story in the period when American interest in Vietnam was beginning to intensify. While the war is not the central focus of "Low Men in Yellow Coats," this story both provides the transition from King's usual genres and sets certain standards against which characters in the other stories will be tested. Ted's struggle against those who wish to destroy the world is a fictional conflict, and his heroism is a conscious act that connects him to the mythic heroes of such works as those in the Dark Tower series. Bobby's actions are like those of the men in Vietnam. He saves Carol in an automatic response to her situation. He passes a physical test but fails the one requiring a moral choice. He does not sacrifice himself. The rest of the stories, except for the final epilogue, repeat these actions in the context of Vietnam. Pete helps carry

Stokely to safety, and he stays in school and saves himself. Both Willie and Sully earn their Silver Stars carrying soldiers to safety, but neither sacrifices himself to save the Vietnamese woman Malenfant impales. The Vietnam genre allows King to examine the nature of heroism in relation to historical situations rather than the more traditional genre patterns of his other fiction. The personal narratives provide specific points of view from those who opposed the war, such as Pete and Carol, to those who believed in it, like Sully. These perspectives give *Hearts in Atlantis* a broader perspective on American culture and the effects of the war than would have been possible with a single point of view. King uses the variety of personal narratives prevalent in the Vietnam genre to expand his examination of this war. He can present conflicting approaches to the conflict, which is an accurate reflection of the way the war was experienced in the United States.

The introduction of Vietnam into his fiction also affects the relationship between past and present in these narratives. His characters may be haunted by ghosts from the past, but these ghosts are linked to historical events that remove them from the scary creatures that inhabit the horror genre. As in other Vietnam narratives, the people of that country are largely ignored. The concern is for how the country and its people affected the Americans who fought there. *Mamasan* is clearly a psychological projection of a veteran and stands for the guilt Sully feels about his activities on one day in Vietnam. Even as an apparition, she is not developed as a character in the way that the ghosts are in a novel like *Bag of Bones*. Past and present are set against the larger concerns of American history. King's adoption of the Vietnam literature genre in *Hearts in Atlantis* allows him to approach his fiction in a different manner. He retains many of the elements of the rest of his fiction, but he uses this shift to examine both form and content in a broader context. The narrative associated with the Vietnam genre lets him divide the book into five stories with five points of view. The introduction of concerns associated with this war gives him the opportunity to challenge traditional genre views of heroism. King uses the shift in genre to reflect on his use of other genres and to deal with issues that might not be possible for him to examine in the context of his use of horror and fantasy.

8

The Girl Who Loved Tom Gordon
(1999)

In the traditional horror story the central character or group of characters must face an evil force that is only gradually understood. The naming and defining of the supernatural horror aid in its destruction. Many of Stephen King's works feature young people dealing with the paranormal. The young have not lost the ability to give credence to an imaginary world since much that happens in the grown-up world seems irrational. In *'Salem's Lot*, for example, a young boy helps the adults understand the vampires they must conquer because his youth allows him to believe in a world that adults find hard to accept. In *The Girl Who Loved Tom Gordon*, King has his protagonist face natural forces that have the same power to destroy and terrorize as do the supernatural. This time her beliefs remain grounded in the actual, but it is her acceptance of the possible reality of her fantasies that allows her to survive. The sentence that opens the novel sets out the challenge young Patricia McFarland must face. "The world had teeth and it could bite you with them any time it wanted" (9). Her obstacles originate in nature, but, for her, they will require the same courage and faith that allow those faced with the supernatural to succeed.

A major source of Trisha's strength is suggested by the title. Tom Gordon was, at the time, a relief pitcher for the Boston Red Sox, King's favorite team. King organizes the book like a baseball game. Trisha's trials follow the chronology of pregame, nine innings, and postgame. He also includes further divisions such as the top of the seventh, the seventh inning stretch, and the top and bottom of the ninth. This organization both reflects the importance of baseball to the novel and gives the reader clues about the pacing of the events in the story.

As Trisha's condition deteriorates, the reader knows the conclusion is near by following the inning markers. The baseball structure also allows King the opportunity to view the game from the outside. In the same way that the game is broadcast to Trisha during her struggles in the woods, King uses the traditions of sports broadcasting to present the story. His narrative includes both the play by play and the color commentary familiar to the fan. As the play-by-play announcer, King tracks Trisha's progress and her trials. As the color commentator, he moves outside of her perspective to give the reader background on the young girl and information about events outside of her knowledge.

PLOT DEVELOPMENT

Just as in a sportscast, King opens *The Girl Who Loved Tom Gordon* by setting up the game. He immediately introduces the players and the conflict. Trisha is safe in her mother's van at 10:00 on a June morning. In half an hour she is lost in the woods because, as she presents it, she needed to pee. In another half hour Trisha knows she is in serious trouble. King then turns to the background of the players. Trisha really doesn't need to relieve herself as much as she wants to get away from the constant fighting between her mother and her brother. By indicating the complexity behind the decisions that lead to her predicament, King engages the reader in a sympathetic relationship with the young girl. A home team can commit an error without losing the love of a fan. Trisha makes a mistake, but the reader understands and still cares about her. Trisha is actually lost in a larger sense before she even leaves her mother's van. She is caught in the turmoil of her parents' year-old divorce. Her brother, Pete, cannot accept their move away from their father, who lives in suburban Boston, to southern Maine. Pete's inability to adjust to a new school is a constant source of conflict. Quilla Anderson, Trisha's mother, thinks that Saturday outings will make her relationship with her son better, and the choice for this particular Saturday will prove to be the ultimate disaster.

In addition to setting up the situation, King introduces the players in the pregame. While they are not exactly organized as opposing teams, Trisha's mother and brother are not seen as supporting her as either daughter or sister. While no one can really join Trisha in her struggle in the wilderness, three characters who have both real and imaginary components help her survive. Tom Gordon is the most important of these. Trisha wears a batting practice jersey with his number, 36, and a baseball cap with his signature that her father, Larry McFarland, got for her. Gordon is her hero. He does his job so well because he has "icewater in his veins" (15) as her father, who also likes him, says. Her other human support is her best friend, Pepsi Robichaud. King also introduces Trisha's doll, Mona, also called Moanie Balogna by her father. The doll remains in the van, but Trisha will think of her during her time in the woods.

King ends the pregame by setting up the situation for the actual game. Trisha already tries to escape the fighting between her mother and brother by retreating into her favorite fantasy, a chance meeting with Tom Gordon. In her reverie he significantly tells her he's a little lost and asks for directions. While King introduces the game the reader has no idea of how it will be played or what will be the outcome.

The first inning begins in the parking lot. Even though King has already set up the events in the pregame show, the real broadcast begins when the players take the field. The game starts in the parking lot as Quilla goes through a final check of the equipment for their hike and leads them to a starting point on their particular piece of the Appalachian Trail in western Maine. From the moment they set out the fighting has consequences for Trisha. She doesn't check for bug spray because it might give Pete an opportunity to start arguing with their mother again. But she only delays the inevitable.

They set out on the trail establishing the pattern that will lead to Trisha's getting lost: mother and son fight while the daughter vainly tries to get their attention. Trisha stops to pee just after they pass a fork in the trail. She opts for the less traveled branch for privacy and walks off that trail to relieve herself. Her mother and brother do not notice that she is no longer with them. In order to get back to them Trisha thinks she can take a shortcut to the main trail rather than going back to the fork. Her first play creates the situation that will control the game. Trisha never returns to the trail.

The second inning opens with Trisha searching for the North Conway branch of the Appalachian Trail. Gradually through this inning and the next she realizes that she is lost. She is not on the path, and she is no longer safe. The tearing of a small hole in her Red Sox shirt is a significant moment in her growing awareness of her situation. The shirt that is her talisman has been damaged, but a dirty torn shirt also can be a result of playing the game. She operates according to a game plan, moving from marker to marker in attempt to travel in a straight line, but her game plan is flawed because she doesn't know the direction of her journey. While the second inning only signals early moments in a game that will run at least nine, Trisha's awareness of her situation calls into question the possibility of completing the game. She realizes that she is alone outside of the rules and boundaries of playing fields that she understands. She almost falls down a cliff. When she avoids immediate death she is attacked by other elements such as bugs. In the early innings she must assess the dangers she faces and devise the means to survive them.

She is over a fourth of the way into the game in the top of the fourth inning. Just as the middle innings test the players so Trisha demonstrates her resources at this time. She deals with a dwindling food and water supply and makes a discovery that is key to her survival. She has taken her Walkman radio with her, and she finds she will be able pick up the Red Sox/Yankee game on the Castle Rock radio station when it is broadcast that evening. She also hears the radio report about her being lost. She has learned certain skills about survival from her parents.

Her mother has always been interested in nature, and her father loves Tom Gordon and teaches her about his belief not in God but in the Subaudible, those things that are so constant in our lives that we don't hear them—like the furnace and the pipes. He doesn't believe in a proactive God but in something, a force that keeps most things going. Her bond with Tom Gordon is strengthened when she listens to the game in the dark. He comes in to save the game at the top of the ninth, and Trisha relates her survival to his success. King as the commentator moves out of her world to tell the reader how the search is going and how her parents are doing.

Unfortunately Trisha is nine miles west of where the searchers think she should be. Like the sportscaster, King inserts this information to keep the reader aware of the totality of the situation. Tom Gordon does get the save and ends the game with a characteristic gesture. Unlike Trisha's father he does believe in God and points at the sky briefly. Trisha imitates this gesture. It connects her to Tom Gordon, but it also makes her understand just how alone she really is.

The bottom of the fourth extends the solitude of her first night in the woods. King introduces a new element at this point; something else is alive in the woods. It comes close to her when she sleeps and even seems to communicate telepathically with her sleeping mother, who stirs at this point. While Trisha senses this danger, she also feels that Tom Gordon guards her. In this pivotal inning, King establishes the forces that will fight for control of Trisha's life: her own will to survive, those things she has learned from her parents, and the forces of good and evil in the world. Evil is wild and natural, while good is connected to humanity, civilization, and skill at playing the game.

The fifth inning is the heart of the game. As King tells us, Trisha's situation worsens, and rather than living she is just attempting to survive. Only the strength of her determination propels her onward. And her other inner resources provide the means for her survival. She talks to Tom Gordon, passing the time by telling him everything she sees and feels. She can also appreciate the rare experiences only possible in such solitude when she comes upon beavers who remind her of illustrations from *The Wind in the Willows*, positive nonthreatening nature. She remembers from her mother and grandmother that Fiddlehead ferns are edible. She enjoys them until she comes on the remains of a deer marked by the claws of the thing that watches her.

Her thirst forces her to drink water. This night she suffers from the water. As she listens to the game she vomits and has diarrhea. She is ill, and the Red Sox lose. Tom Gordon does not play. The search also goes wrong when someone calls the police to claim she has been abducted. But Tom Gordon comes to her in the night. Her vision of him and his absolute stillness transfers to her own misery as she tries to use stillness to rid herself of the shakes.

When she wakens in the morning she is better. It is the sixth inning. The pattern of her life in the woods has been established, but each day is also different. Berries give Trisha energy, and views of fawns and their mother and butterflies in a clearing restore her soul. But the butterflies are also connected to the dark side of nature, a vision that is identified both with the creature that haunts her and the God of the Lost. As she is entranced by a vision, both white and black robed figures appear to her. White is connected to her father and the Subaudible, forms that provide no help. The black robed figure turns out to be a wasp-priest who presents a negative view of the world. Trisha finally decides her visions are a result of the berries she ate. But the real images that follow the dream are even more upsetting. Once out of the clearing she finds the remains of a fawn and claw marks on a tree. As she nears the end of the game both real and imaginary images, the result of lack of food and bad water, add to her distress.

By the top of the seventh inning Trisha's health is failing. She now has a cough and fever. However, a dream of Tom Gordon in a meadow with her and a post with a rusty ringbolt point to a future event still hidden from the reader. Tom expresses the possibility of divine intervention, especially in the bottom of the ninth. When things look very bad for Trisha's survival, King uses Tom Gordon to provide hope for both the young girl and the reader. While the thing in the woods still watches and Tom tells her she will have to deal with it at some point, Trisha's instincts take over and she catches a fish and eats it raw. King both gives the reader hope and then takes it away. The fish gives Trisha strength, but she makes a bad decision. She chooses not to climb a ridge where she would have seen signs of civilization and instead turns further into the wilderness.

King must continue this structure of hope and fear in order to have Trisha play out the game to its end. The end of the game is where Tom Gordon shines, and Trisha must get there as well. In the bottom of the seventh she is further away from help, but she survives the fever. Tom Gordon gets two saves on the road in games that Trisha is able to hear on her radio. The world has almost given up searching for her, but she walks on. Finally she finds a stump in a meadow with a rusty ringbolt. Tom, who has become her imaginary companion, tells her that she dreamed of this post. She realizes she has finally found a sign of civilization, part of a gate that leads her to a path and the ruts of an old road.

While Trisha may be literally out of the woods, the game is not over; it is only the eighth inning. She may be closer to civilization, but the beast that has been following her is also nearer. She takes shelter in the remains of an old truck, but something digs a circle around it during the night as if marking territory. The end of the game becomes a contest between the opposing forces that have fought over Trisha for the whole book. The beast follows her as she struggles to emulate her hero and win the game in the ninth inning. The top of the ninth sets up the end of the game. She is exhausted, but she finds the game on her radio. Her cough is worse, and something watches her from the edge of the woods.

The bottom of the ninth inning provides all of the challenges that a pitcher like Tom Gordon faces when trying to save the game. Everything seems to be going against Trisha. She begins to cough up blood; she is so tired she sleeps by the side of the road; the batteries in the radio die, and she almost loses the radio. But just like a pitcher who selects the right pitch, she selects the correct turn in the road. In the save-the-game situation the beast finally appears. It is a bear—a real creature, not a creation of her imagination. But he still comes for her. She finds the strength to imitate Tom Gordon and his stillness and takes her Walkman to throw at the beast. At the same moment a man, Travis Herrick, trying to poach deer out of season sees her and the bear. Because she does not move the bear does not charge her. As she throws the Walkman she gives Herrick a clear shot. She hits the bear, as does the bullet, and it runs into the woods while she calls strike three. As the man catches her she tries to claim the save and then faints.

The postgame moves the reader and Trisha back into the world she left when she strayed off the path. King, the commentator, summarizes both Trisha's dreams and the reactions of her family. Her pneumonia makes talk impossible, but she manages to get her father to give her the baseball cap. She reproduces Tom Gordon's gesture after a save by touching the visor and pointing up to the ceiling. Her father understands, and the game is over. The reader knows that Trisha's experience has been more than a game. Baseball may have helped her survive, but her own inner resources go beyond those needed to succeed in a sport. Just as Tom Gordon's gesture acknowledges a belief in something more important than his role as a player, Trisha's determination to keep going demonstrates an inner strength and an awareness of the forces that reside in nature and humanity.

CHARACTER DEVELOPMENT

While there are few characters in *The Girl Who Loved Tom Gordon*, Trisha's interactions with the natural world and with those people she has left behind form the core of the novel. The plot only occasionally focuses on the people waiting and looking for her, but these people and their lives are always a part of her world. Trisha is a product of both her parents, and the information and beliefs they have transmitted become part of the personality that ensures her survival. In addition, Tom Gordon, whose imaginary presence travels with her, and the bear that tracks her are integral parts of her journey.

Patricia McFarland

Trisha is nine years old on that day in June when she leaves the path and gets lost. At first she seems to be the typical child of divorced parents, more aware of the adult world than other children of her age. She lives with her mother and her brother, Pete. Her connection to her father is symbolized by the Boston Red Sox jersey she wears and her love of Tom Gordon. She rides in the backseat of the car with her doll, Mona, called Moanie Balogna by her father, and tries to avoid listening to the argument between her mother, Quilla Anderson, and her brother by thinking about Tom Gordon. She has admitted to her best friend, Pepsi Robichaud, that she thinks the player is attractive. Unfortunately for her, the family argument continues as they leave the car and go on the trail. As the youngest member of the family Trisha feels helpless and ignored. These feelings lead to her almost fatal error of leaving the trail.

Her initial choice to move off the path and not call out to her mother and brother is the result of her youth. But once she fully understands her situation when she is lost, other aspects of her character come to the fore. Away from the conflicts created by the adult world she must rely on inner strengths to survive. Trisha actually grows more independent the longer she is lost. She uses the skills she has learned from her parents: the knowledge of natural lore from her mother and the courage of Tom Gordon from her father. Until almost the end she makes choices that lead her further into the wilderness. But she does not give up even when she must face her childhood terrors alone in the dark at night pursued by some unknown creature.

Trisha is a modern child. She may have learned about edible plants from her mother and grandmother, but she also lives because of the technology of her Walkman. Listening to baseball games comforts her and provides the example of Tom Gordon for inspiration. She uses mud as an old-fashioned remedy for bug bites, but she stops the bear with the radio. Even in the midst of her worst days she avoids panic and has the maturity to appreciate privileged moments when she comes across beavers or deer that she would not have been able to see in other circumstances. She also deals with questions of faith, as she must reconcile her father's view of the Subaudible with Tom Gordon's faith and the challenges of the beast that stalks her. We never forget that she is a child, but she demonstrates a credible maturity that allows us to also believe in her survival.

The Family

Trisha's family may be responsible for her getting lost, and unlike many in such stories, they are only indirectly involved in her rescue. They give her skills that enable her to live in the wilderness, but they are not really present for much of the story. Aside from the opening they are visible only in Trisha's memories or in brief scenes of the search. However they do remain connected. At the same moment Trisha hears a branch snap, her sleeping mother moves and awakens, aware of her daughter. Pete is even more restless. He dreams of the moment when he realized Trisha was gone. She disappears so completely for him that he almost feels like he never had a sister.

Even though Pete's inability to deal with the changes brought on by the divorce precipitate Trisha's getting lost, he is not really connected to her survival. He acts as the catalyst that precipitates the crisis. As the older child he also represents the deeper damage children experience when their parents divorce. He wants to remain with his father rather than go with his mother, and he hates his new school. At the old school he was king of the computer club nerds. In his group he was safe from other students. In the new school there is no such group to join. The only friend he is able to make moves away because of a divorce. He is alone, an object of ridicule. The solitude he suffers at school leads to the argument that provokes Trisha into leaving the trail. They are connected by the effect of the divorce, a separation from other people.

Tom Gordon

Tom Gordon is both a real and an imaginary character in the novel. King acknowledges this difference in his postscript to the book. He also points out that there is always a fictional element in fans' perceptions of famous people. But the gesture this player uses when he gets a save is real. In addition to being Trisha's imaginary companion and inspiration, Tom Gordon also takes on a symbolic function. He counters Larry McFarland's belief in the Subaudible, a force for the good that exists to keep things going well most of the time. Tom Gordon represents a force that is closer to the traditional perception of God. In Trisha's encounter with the images that haunt her, the first white hooded figure comes from the God of Tom Gordon even though he looks like her science teacher. The gesture of pointing up to the sky is another means of acknowledging a divine presence.

The pitcher also figures in the dream of the post that ultimately proves true and becomes Trisha's guide to the road and her salvation. In a kind of modern-day version of religion or superstition, she ties his saves to her survival. The stillness he achieves when he pitches becomes emblematic of courage and skill in response to difficult situations. Trisha achieves this same stillness before her successful pitch when she hits the bear with the Walkman. Tom Gordon also represents a stability for the child of a divorce, a connection to the absent father and a code of conduct beyond the divisive arguments of parents and siblings.

The Bear

The beast that is finally identified as a bear is also both real and imaginary in the book. The beast that tracks Trisha leaves a trail of destruction that she can see, but it also exists on an almost supernatural level. In *The Girl Who Loved Tom Gordon*, this beast is as close as King gets to introducing a traditional horror figure. While the beast leaves claw marks on trees and kills deer, it stalks Trisha like a figure from nightmares rather than nature. The reader wonders why a real bear wouldn't have attacked immediately instead of haunting the young girl. And its true nature is only revealed to the reader at the same time that Trisha sees it. For both the reader and Trisha, its reality is in question until the end. In her vision it is represented by the black robed wasp-priest, who also states that he comes from the God of the Lost.

If Tom Gordon denotes God and civilization, the bear stands for wild nature and evil. The natural world is not inherently evil, but the existence of such creatures illustrates the dangers in straying from the path. The real bear is part of the world that can bite, nature beyond hiking paths and the toy woods of Trisha's mother. The bear is also the ultimate test for Trisha. At the end of the book she is able to face the worst that nature can present and conquer it. In the final confrontation, Tom Gordon and all that he represents win out over the forces of evil.

ALTERNATIVE READING: REGIONALISM

"Regionalism" is a term in literature applied to the representation of various elements associated with a specific place. Regional literature can use speech mannerisms, beliefs, habits, and local lore to depict both the specific and the universal in writing. In regional writing the area is integral to the work and the location cannot be changed without damaging its integrity. While this term can be associated with literature anywhere in the world, a version of it known as Local Color Writing became a dominant force in the United States toward the end of the nineteenth century. King is not usually categorized as a regional writer, but the majority of his fiction is set in New England and more specifically in Maine. He creates new towns and renames existing ones as he presents his own version of this state. Derry, the setting for many novels, is really Bangor, and Castle Rock, where Trisha's family waits for news when she is lost, is an invention located near his childhood home in Durham. Nathaniel Hawthorne found this area an ideal setting for supernatural events, and King updates this world in his fiction. In recent fiction he has moved from imaginary to real horrors that seem to foment in this area. In *Dolores Claiborne*, a small island off the coast of Maine is a site for incest and murder. *The Girl Who Loved Tom Gordon* further develops many of the elements of King's approach to regionalism.

King often features the smaller towns of New England in his fiction. These isolated communities are perfect settings for horror fiction. People can disappear without creating a stir in the larger world, and these insular communities are perfect breeding grounds for the prejudice and greed that King's fiction examines. Trisha's mother has moved from suburban Boston to southern Maine after her divorce. The small-town mentality of Sanford creates the climate that generates the ongoing argument between Pete and his mother. The search for Trisha becomes derailed when a vindictive anonymous caller tells the state police that a man called Francis Raymond Mazzerole has abducted her.

The region also has enough wilderness to make credible Trisha's not being found. There are no markers to indicate her crossing over into New Hampshire. At one point she does not climb a ridge and instead heads in a direction where there is nothing except wilderness between her and Montreal, four hundred miles to the north. The area is dense enough for bears to roam freely. The isolation of the region fosters the kind of self-sufficiency Trisha demonstrates. Even the poacher who finds her is typical of an area where such activity can be carried out with impunity.

New England is the site of some of the oldest settlements and the most modern regionalism in the United States. While the favorite basketball and baseball teams retain Boston in their names, the football team is the New England Patriots. The Red Sox games are broadcast throughout the region. One can cross state lines, move from suburban Boston to southern Maine and not have to change allegiance to one's team. Tom Gordon is both a member of the Boston Red Sox and a modern embodiment of the virtues associated with the early settlers, as can be seen in his famous gesture at the end of the game. Trisha, too, faces the basic conflict between good and evil associated with authors like Hawthorne in a landscape where the lines between real and imaginary events may blur. In *The Girl Who Loved Tom Gordon*, King turns to baseball to develop yet another element in his presentation of his region, extending the virtues of earlier settlers to another American tradition.

9

Dreamcatcher
(2001)

Dreamcatcher is the first major work written by Stephen King after the accident that changed his life. In the author's note that follows the novel, he acknowledges the pleasure that writing this novel gave him. While he was in pain, he also remembered the "sublime release we find in vivid dreams" (619). He blends pain and dreams in this book that both extends and develops the themes and structures of his recent work. While King remains within the boundaries of genre fiction in *Dreamcatcher*, he demonstrates how those boundaries can be expanded. He is immersed in the popular culture that underlies his work in genre fiction and is able to transcend it and transform it.

As with so much of his work, this novel contains echoes of the past. King always remembers the world he has created in his fiction. But this time the role of memory becomes one of its central themes. No one can leave her or his past behind because it defines the present. For those who have remained faithful readers of King's work, the fragments of other novels that appear in a new work become part of the reader's history and memory as well. Those who have followed his career have their own events to add to the experience of reading, such as what they were doing or where they were the first time they encountered the imaginary town of Derry. For the first-time reader who begins with a new King novel, there is the anticipation of a new world to be discovered beyond this book. And the experience of reading *Dreamcatcher* will also become a part of each reader's memory.

This novel seems to return to familiar King territory. Four men who have been friends since childhood meet each year at the hunting cabin called Hole in the Wall that belonged to the father of one of them. While their lives have diverged they are bound together by several keys events from their youth. The image of four boyhood friends recalls King's short story "The Body," made into the film *Stand By Me*. Many of his novels deal with boys on the verge of adolescence who face critical events that will change their lives, from *'Salem's Lot* to *Hearts in Atlantis*.

But these boys are now adults in their late thirties. Some have lives that are more successful than others. They must all face a new crisis together. King explores the trajectories of people's lives. He wants to know the difference between those who give up and those who continue to fight; those who succumb and those who triumph. Ultimately life is a struggle between those factors we have been born with and those choices we make along the way. While the novel's story is compelling as the characters become enmeshed in an alien invasion, the decisions they make and the qualities they demonstrate make this a novel where character is as important as plot.

PLOT DEVELOPMENT

While the overall structure of *Dreamcatcher* may at first seem familiar to the reader of King's fiction, the organization of the novel gradually shifts until it is transformed into the most complex of any of his works. It opens with what becomes a prologue and then is divided into three main parts followed by an epilogue. The novel is further segmented into twenty-one chapters numbered consecutively through the three parts. Each chapter is further divided into numbered sections. The major divisions follow the action of the novel but not a linear time frame. Memories intrude, taking characters back to key points in their lives. As the characters' telepathic powers develop, many events occur at the same time: people can follow thoughts and movements of other groups at different locations, forcing the reader to track both locations and thoughts while the action moves toward the climax.

King titles the prefatory material which usually contains quotations that set the tone for the work, "FIRST, THE NEWS" (9). The news consists of a series of newspaper headlines dealing with the appearance of aliens and flying saucers including some from Roswell, New Mexico, a location so famous for its association with UFOs that it became the title of a television series. In addition to the usual images of spacecraft, lights in the sky, and gray men with big black eyes, there are also reports of a strange red weed and unexplained episodes of food poisoning. The last report comes from the Derry, Maine, paper and tells of mysterious lights in nearby Jefferson Tract. These headlines establish the context for the novel. The reader realizes that aliens will pose some kind of threat in *Dreamcatcher*.

The prologue sets up a narrative structure that should be familiar to the experienced reader. King is master of the technique of foreshadowing coming events to create suspense and raise a series of questions. This technique immediately involves the reader in the novel, both in anticipation of future events and in attempts to put together information to answer the questions raised. The heading of this section, "SSDD," is an example of this technique. The meaning of these letters, repeated many times in this section, looms as a puzzle behind its events. King tells us these letters are the motto for the group and then gradually introduces the members. But even the makeup of the group becomes a part of the puzzle because its numbers change. The composition goes from four to five to four. The path of the novel is also suggested when King states that life got darker when they became four again. The passage of time will be an important element, and it will not have a positive effect on these four characters.

King uses different instants in their lives to introduce each one of them. He moves from Beaver in 1988 to close to the present. Beaver is in a bar but not with his true friends. He only sees them once a year in November. Pete, the car salesman who dreamed of being an astronaut, helps a woman find her car keys in 1993 by using a strange talent that he has for locating things by waving his finger in front of his face. Henry, the psychiatrist, treats a particular patient in 1998. He pays more attention to his own thoughts of the annual hunting trip with Jonesy, Pete, and Beaver that will start the next day. The final introduction of Jonesy describes the events in his life on the day of the accident that will change his life in March of 2001, a date that occurs immediately after the actual publication of the novel.

We finally learn that SSDD means "same shit different day" (34), a phrase that really erases time. Information anticipating the accident appears throughout this segment. At the same time earlier questions are already answered. We learn the fate of Henry's patient. And new questions are raised when Henry feels the need to go to Derry to see the fifth member of the group, who has remained a boy. All of the friends seem to have some kind of special power. Henry warns Jonesy to be careful. Another alert about Mr. Gray pops into Jonesy's mind. But none of these alarms will be effective.

The first part of the novel moves ahead to the hunting trip in November 2001. This part is titled "Cancer," the word King wanted to use for the novel itself. As he states in the author's note, his wife persuaded him to change his mind. While the preface covers several years in the lives of the characters, the rest of the book will actually take place over the span of about twenty-four hours of actual time. However, it will move back and forth over a much longer period in their lives. The opening confirms the pattern of raising questions and anticipating future events that King has already begun in the prologue. With a thought that he returns to at many points in the novel, Jonesy wishes that he had shot the man named Richard McCarthy when he first saw him and thought he was a deer. This action might have saved all of them.

Once this suspenseful piece of information is presented, we learn that the friends are enjoying their annual hunting trip. Pete and Henry have gone to Gosselin's Market for supplies. Beaver is hunting, and Jonesy, who has really lost his taste for killing deer, is still sitting in a stand near the cabin with his rifle. We also learn that Jonesy is not as mobile as the others. He was hit by a car on that day in March and suffered a fractured skull, two broken ribs, and a shattered hip. At this point we do not know exactly how close to death he came, because he does not know that his heart stopped twice in the ambulance. But he does know that this accident has changed his life. The events of the next few minutes will change it even more.

The man he fails to shoot shows up at the cabin, behaving in a very strange manner. He seems to be disoriented and exhausted by being lost in the woods. He is missing four teeth from what otherwise looks like a perfect mouth, and he has a strange red patch on his cheek. His symptoms are our first introduction to the effects of encounters with an alien life force that, by the end of the novel, will be very familiar. At first, however, they are just a series of clues that the reader may connect to the headlines that open *Dreamcatcher*. Once he is in the cabin with Jonesy, the man does notice a dreamcatcher hanging from the ceiling of the main room. Jonesy explains it is an Indian charm that is used to keep away nightmares. Beav returns, and they both notice the strong, odd-smelling farts the man cannot avoid making. There are points in his story that also do not make sense. The man is ill, and they put him to sleep in one of the bedrooms.

At the same time that these events occur, Henry and Pete are on the road back from the store in the midst of a snowstorm. The trip reveals character and plot information. Henry is suicidal, Pete is an alcoholic, and Mr. Gosselin is concerned about the strange lights in the sky and missing hitting hunters. Two events happen at almost the same time. Henry has to swerve to miss hitting a woman sitting in the middle of the road and overturns the Scout he is driving, and McCarthy wakes up and goes to the bathroom. These two events establish different paths for each of the pair of friends. Pete injures his leg in the crash, but he and Henry manage to drag the woman to a lean-to for some shelter from the storm. Both men talk about Duddits after seeing a child at the store with Down's syndrome. They provide more information about this person who had once been one of them, a clue to their past. We learn that at a defining moment in their childhood they behaved well. Henry decides to try to hike the ten miles to the Hole in the Wall to get the snowmobile.

Back at the cabin McCarthy does not come out of the bathroom. Jonesy and Beav play cribbage and recall playing the game when they were little. Duddits couldn't play, but he moved the pegs. While strange things happen outside the cabin, such as huge numbers of animals passing by or a helicopter overhead, the sounds from the bathroom are even odder. All evidence leads the two men to be concerned about their strange guest. Before they finally break into the bathroom, King maintains the suspense by returning to Pete and Henry and further information about Duddits. Through the technique of moving back and forth between these characters and between past and present, King can introduce back story, keep the tension high, and provide connections between past and present that are central to plot and theme.

Pete cannot stand being alone with the woman, and he also cannot stop thinking about the beer left in the overturned Scout three-quarters of a mile away. Even with his bad leg he sets out to get the beer. When he finally reaches the vehicle he thinks back to his lost dreams and, as he drinks his second beer, to the day the friends met Duddits. He was in eighth grade, a year behind the other three. King tells us that at this point in 1978 in Derry, the young Duddits was still a half hour in their future, leading us to anticipate learning about this life-changing encounter.

The boys talk about the upcoming hunting trip, their first to the Hole in the Wall, and don't even notice passing Mary M. Snowe school, also known as "The Retard Academy." We know this information is important. We can put together some of the details, but King still draws us forward by withholding more until the last moment. The boys are drawn to the abandoned Tracker Brothers Depot by the possibility of seeing a picture of the Homecoming Queen, Tina Jean Schlossinger, with her skirt raised and no underpants. They don't have to actually enter the building. All they have to do is look through the window. At this moment King returns to the present to delay the revelation.

Pete walks back to the shelter and once again thinks of the past. But King also tells us about Henry jogging toward the cabin and worrying about Jonesy and Beav, who he senses are in trouble. The telepathic connections between the characters increase the tension. We too worry about the two men at the cabin. This time Henry's mind provides the point of view for the events in 1978. Henry senses trouble as they approach the building and find a Scooby Doo lunch box on the road. They hear screams and laughter as three high school boys surround a younger boy they are forcing to eat dog-turds. On the wall behind them are the words "no bounce, no play," which will become their catchphrase. In this unequal confrontation, the younger boys manage to overcome the older ones and rescue the child, Douglas Cavell, who is known as Duddits. They are willing to risk being beaten up to save this innocent victim. King suggests that there is more to the story. We realize that some questions have been answered, but new ones are raised. Beav takes the boy in his arms and stops his crying by singing.

Once again King returns to the present for a moment as Henry receives images from the cabin and of Pete in trouble because he returned to the Scout. Then we are back in October of 1978. Before they take Duddits to his house, meet his mother, and begin a friendship that will last as long at they remain in Derry, they do see the picture. It is not the homecoming queen, and they only see underpants. Henry returns to the present aware that something horrible has happened. He hears the noise of a snowmobile and hides in the woods. He sees someone he knows who is in the midst of a red cloud pass by. He is aware that one friend is dead and another is transformed into a movie star. While Henry understands this information, we will not really know what it means until later. We are also puzzled by what might have happened to lead to these events.

King takes us back to Jonesy and Beav, a move into the immediate past that becomes part of the pattern of time shifts that are both the result of simultaneous events and telepathic communication. The two men finally open the door to the bathroom. There is blood everywhere. McCarthy is dead with a huge hole in his rear. Jonesy knows there is something horrible in the toilet. He is a great fan of horror films and thinks something he has seen may help them. He tells Beav to sit on the toilet seat cover while he gets friction tape from the shed to tape it down. We know that something terrible is going to happen, but we must watch it unfold. While Beav waits for Jonesy he too thinks back to 1978 and

Duddits. He remembers the reaction of Roberta, the boy's mother, and how they all become friends and volunteer to walk the boy to school. The friends do this for the next five years until they begin to go their separate ways. Again King provides answers and then new questions when Beav raises the name of Josie Rinkenhauer and another event from the past.

The novel returns to the present. Beav thinks Jonesy is taking too long. He becomes restless. He loves to chew on toothpicks, and his mother has told him they will be the death of him. He has dropped his supply on the floor just out of reach. As he leans over to get one, he releases just enough pressure from the lid for a horrible weasel-looking creature with big black eyes, sharp teeth, and a strong reddish gold tail to emerge and attack him. Beav struggles. Jonesy, who finally finds the tape, runs back into the cabin and sees Beav's face being eaten as the tail wraps itself about his friend's waist. Beav dies, and Jonesy traps the thing in the bathroom. As it tries to escape, Jonesy turns to run and is confronted by a tall, gray man whose head explodes, releasing a cloud of particles that Jonesy inhales. We now know what has happened in the cabin.

King broadens the scope of his story by introducing information about events occurring beyond this specific tract of land in northern Maine. We learn that Duddits is now very ill, dying of leukemia. We see on his television news coverage of the cover-up of the landing of the aliens. We have enough information to put major facts together about the creatures and a ship that has crashed in the woods. We have evidence of the effects of the aliens on people we have come to know and like. King gradually provides further information about the cancer that the aliens seem to bring, a reddish-gold substance that grows on its host and provides telepathic powers.

King then introduces the final component of the novel's structure, the presence of the military who have quarantined the area and are attempting to contain the menace presented by the aliens. Chief among them are a madman called Kurtz and his second in command, Owen Underhill. In addition to killing gray men around the downed spacecraft, these men are part of an operation to round up anyone in the area who might be contaminated by contact with the reddish-gold substance. Their headquarters is at Gosselin's store. They call the alien fungus "Ripley" after the character portrayed by Sigourney Weaver in the *Alien* films. The military presence eventually leads to new alliances among the friends.

Jonesy, driven by Mr. Gray, who has now taken over his body, evades capture. He finds Pete, who has been wounded fighting off the weasel that emerged from the woman's body and takes him on the snowmobile.

Pete is useful because of his ability to locate things. He is able to direct the snowmobile north to the main highway. Once he serves his purpose, the gray man forces Jonesy to leave him to die. At the same time Henry is captured as he approaches Gosselin's store on cross-country skis he got from the shed at the Hole in the Wall. He had to set the camp on fire to destroy the weasel and prevent its eggs from spreading from the cabin. Owen and Kurtz argue, and Kurtz no longer trusts his officer. Henry manages to contact Owen. They communicate both telepathically and verbally. King connects characters in new combinations as the story, and its timelines intensify. Henry convinces the officer that the real threat comes from Mr. Gray, who has escaped and is the Typhoid Mary who will carry the alien infection to the world beyond the quarantine. Henry hopes some of Jonesy may remain inside the body taken over by the alien. The rest of the novel becomes an exciting chase among three elements who keep track of each other through telepathy. Henry and Owen set out after Mr. Gray; and Kurtz and his new aide, Freddy Johnson, follow Owen, whom Kurtz wants to destroy. From this point the various kinds of communications between the characters and the events from the past that have formed them are woven together into a complex pattern where all are connected like the strings in a dreamcatcher.

Henry knows they have to have Duddits with them. He realizes that Duddits is their dreamcatcher; he is the force that has united them all of these years and increased the telepathic connections among them. Kurtz takes along two soldiers infected with the fungus to use to track Owen and Henry. Jonesy has retreated into his mind, especially into those memories he has managed to hide from Mr. Gray. He hopes to find some way to defeat this alien presence. He moves between past and future. He realizes that he stepped off the curb into the path of the car because he saw Duddits in the crowd and went to save him.

His memories turn into a film directed by the alien, and he retreats from the hospital after his accident to that office in the Tracker Brothers Depot with those memories he has retrieved, especially those concerning Duddits. Henry figures out that Mr. Gray is heading toward the Quabbin reservoir that feeds Boston. He has a dog infected with Ripley, which he calls byrum. If he can get the dog into the water the fungus will feed off the body and then spread throughout the country. Another snowstorm makes all travel difficult. Mr. Gray manages to steal a series of vehicles while the two military men drive Humvees. As King juggles the three groups, the reader must keep the various characters and their coming convergence in mind.

Henry and Owen get to Derry and finally convince Roberta to let them take the dying boy/man with them. Duddits knows they are coming and is dressed and waiting. The chase grows more intense. Duddits uses all of his powers to try to hold back Mr. Gray until they can reach him. Jonesy, too, attempts to stop Mr. Gray. Finally they are at the woods near the shaft leading into the reservoir. Kurtz is not far behind. Mr. Gray re-breaks Jonesy's hip while getting the cover partially off of the shaft. He cannot push the dog in. Owen leaves Henry and Duddits in the vehicle. Through Duddits Henry manages to communicate with Jonesy and tells him how they are all connected by the dreamcatcher. Henry tells him it is time to come out. Jonesy should run along the dreamcatcher to meet Henry. Jonesy escapes from Mr. Gray when he finally admits that he and Mr. Gray are one. The weasel comes out of the dying dog. Owen appears and shoots it. Henry manages to communicate that Mr. Gray no longer inhabits Jonesy before Duddits dies.

Meanwhile Freddy and Kurtz arrive. Freddy thinks Henry and Duddits, in the backseat of the Humvee, are already dead and ignores them. Kurtz and Freddy hear shots and wait in the wood to see who will emerge from the shaft. When Owen comes out they kill him, and Freddy shoots Kurtz as he stands over the dying Owen. Freddy dies when he returns to the Humvee and is attacked by the weasel that has come out of the man they used to track Owen. Henry sets fire to the vehicle. In the end he manages to rescue Jonesy. Finally the complex threads of the narrative reach a resolution. King only has to answer a few remaining questions.

The epilogue takes place on Labor Day. Henry is at Jonesy's cottage with his friend's wife and children. The two men have to talk over what they learned during their extensive debriefing. King answers all of the questions he has raised. The fungus and the weasels (and the byrum virus they produce) are not intelligent. The byrus is the product of a race that may be dead. Mr. Gray was able to steal Jonesy's personality, because the teacher saw what he expected to see based on his own experiences, especially the movies he loves. Henry discusses the reality of Duddits. The special qualities he brought to the friends were both good and bad. With him they were able to find a girl who was lost. But under his influence they were also able to dream the destruction of the boy who tormented Duddits in an automobile accident. There is a dreamcatcher hanging in Jonesy's cabin. Aliens will be back at some point but not right now. Henry and Jonesy survive.

CHARACTER DEVELOPMENT

There are two major groups of characters in *Dreamcatcher*, the people who have spent all or part of their lives connected to Duddits and the members of the military who come to Jefferson Tract to contain the menace posed by the aliens. Everyone is faced with a moment of decision. The difference between becoming a hero or a villain is the result of the choices made at critical points in life. In many King novels the characters are pushed forward by earlier events. Their reactions to these events come from their individual personalities shaped by their pasts. In *Dreamcatcher* the idea of choice is foregrounded. People may be the products of their past, but they can grow and develop in the present and thus take control of their futures. King introduces another idea in this novel, the connections that exist between human beings. Some of the ties that bind people together are the result of choices they make, but the relationships that are formed can create a new kind of community.

King contrasts the group formed by the four boys and Duddits with the group created by the military. In both cases both good and bad can emerge from such an association. But the bonds formed by the boys lead them to a higher kind of association that, in the end, transcends their individual problems and helps them save the world from the alien invasion. And the boys never turn on each other or betray each other. The heroic act that brought them together provides the glue that even at times overcomes the death of some of them. While the military group formed in the novel would seem to have the greater good as their goal, individuals cannot blend their identities to form a truly cohesive union.

The Group

Four people remain full members of the group from their youth in Derry through their adult years until their middle thirties, when they encounter the aliens. While they were friends before the incident that defined their future, their meeting with Duddits changes them forever. Duddits is the fifth who comes into their lives for a while and then remains in Derry when they leave. During the course of the novel they discover his true role in their friendship and the positive and negative aspects of their association with him. In their adult lives they have taken different paths, but they continue to remain close friends. They think about Duddits, although they don't really see him anymore. The four never fail to meet each year in November at the Hole in the Wall to hunt. All of them to a greater or lesser extent have a kind of void or emptiness in their adult lives. They also have a kind of psychic connection. Their past puts them in a unique position to combat the alien invasion. The identities of those who survive and those who die suggest a kind of moral judgment.

The two members of the original group who die as a result of contact with the aliens fail because of flaws in their characters. Pete's return trip to the Scout to get beer further injures his leg. And he is so consumed by the need for alcohol that he forgets to get his rifle and has to use more primitive means such as fire to fend off the weasel that emerges from the woman. Beaver cannot resist getting a toothpick and releases the weasel from the toilet. It is not just the habit that defeats him but also his lack of patience.

Duddits also dies as a result of his illness. But his illness can also be seen as a kind of metaphoric symbol of his imperfection. He has provided the center, the point in the dreamcatcher that holds them together as a force for good, but he has also been the source of a destructive dream. The boys save him, and later, with his help, they locate another student from his school in the spring of 1982 just before three of them graduate. Josie Rinkenhauer has fallen into a storm drain. They manage to get her out and return her to her family. But they also have the somewhat suppressed memory of another event.

Not long after they meet Duddits they spend their first week at the Hole in the Wall. They all wake up from a terrible dream, the death of the chief tormentor, Richie Grenadeau, and his cohort in an automobile accident that severs Richie's head. They realize that they have shared Duddits's dream and go to Gosselin's store to call him. He is upset, but he has dreamed his enemies to death so the friends will not have to worry about any reprisals. Once they finally acknowledge and accept Duddits's role in this event they can understand how he operated for both good and bad in their lives.

Two members of the group never really develop much beyond the time that they spend together. Joe "Beaver" Clarendon, with a nickname from a popular television character, still lives near Derry and works as a carpenter. His brief marriage fails, but he remains a basically happy person. He has the bad habit of chewing toothpicks, the habit that costs him his life. He is also known among his friends for his colorful language. He is the one who comforts Duddits after the rescue and sings to make him stop crying. Beaver's father owns the Hole in the Wall and brings the boys there for the first time in 1978. Beav later inherits the cabin. While he does not survive in the novel, he does appear in a talking photograph after his death. Beaver is the first of the four to die.

Pete Moore is the other member of the group who has not changed much as he has grown older. He is the youngest member and was a year behind the others in school. Pete's youthful dreams have never been realized. As a boy his room was filled with images of space exploration, and he wanted to be an astronaut. All that is left of this ambition is a NASA key fob. Pete is a car salesman and an alcoholic who has a unique ability to locate things. He wags his index finger in front of his face in a kind of hypnotic motion and is then able to find a lost object or direction. His talent is valuable in locating Josie, but he also helps the alien escape. His fatal flaw is his alcoholism, which is also one way to deal with lost dreams.

Henry Devlin has become a psychiatrist. King introduces him treating a difficult patient whom he finally offends. Even before the aliens arrive, he knows this will be his last time at the Hole in the Wall. Henry plans to deal with the emptiness in his life by committing suicide. On the trip back from Gosselin's store he thinks over the various methods he might employ. Henry's experiences in the novel help him deal with his past. Once he fully understands the role that Duddits played in their lives, he is able to continue. At the end of *Dreamcatcher*, he still has thoughts of death, but he is able to deal with them. He has lost three fingers through frostbite. No one emerges from an encounter with death unmarked. Henry has learned the art of survival. He has learned to deal with his memories of those who were killed, especially the civilians rounded up by the military. Henry had convinced Owen Underhill to give them a chance, but many had died. He also knows that as long as Duddits was around they were tied into the dreamcatcher.

Jonesy, Gary Ambrose Jones, is a college professor who teaches history. His life is changed twice, the first time by the encounter with Duddits and the second time by his accident and subsequent brush with death. His injuries are similar to those suffered by King, and some of his reaction to the accident can be seen as a reflection of the author's experiences. At first he cannot remember anything leading up to the encounter. Only at the end does he connect it to Duddits. Jonesy thinks he saw his friend, and that image provided the distraction that sent him into the street without first looking around carefully. While the accident may have been a component of those elements that made Jonesy immune to the byrum, his love of horror films enabled Mr. Gray to take the form that he did. The byrum was not intelligent, but

Jonesy saw and experienced the invasion based on his previous contact with the idea of aliens in films. On one level Jonesy was invaded, but on another he created the form that invasion took. He also finds ways to save himself from destruction. The dream world he enters, especially the office he uses, is similar to Audrey's retreat in *The Regulators*. This time the concept of the refuge is developed more fully. The alien used what it could of Jonesy's personality. As Henry explains, Jonesy was immune to the byrum. He only caught an intention (613) that is hard to really describe because it is not of our world. By the end of the novel Jonesy has returned to his old life once again, altered by experience. For a moment a small remnant of the telepathic connection that used to exist unites him with Henry.

Duddits, whose full name is Douglas Cavell, provides the moments that unite the group at the same time that he also is responsible for the event that creates distress among the members. He first encounters the group when Richie Grenadeau and his friends at the Tracker Brothers Depot are threatening him. They think he is an easy target because he is younger than they are and is developmentally challenged. While Duddits does not speak clearly, the friends immediately understand him. What they don't fully appreciate is the way that he holds them together. Only the survivors see Duddits as the dreamcatcher. In this character King expands the role of the different child that he explored with Seth in *The Regulators*. Duddits is much more complex both in his interaction with other characters and as a personality on his own.

At the end of the novel Henry reveals that Duddits actually understood much more of their cribbage game than they thought he did. The boys let him move the pegs, but they thought he did it in a random manner. Henry tells Jonesy that once Pete did something to Duddits that he didn't like, and Pete lost at the game for a long time. Duddits can both save and destroy. Henry feels that he saved him when Freddy passed by the Humvee at the reservoir. Duddits manages to separate Jonesy from Mr. Gray just before he dies. And Duddits also delays Mr. Gray's arrival at the reservoir long enough to let Owen and Henry arrive on time. But Duddits also fed off the more developed anger of the boys to create the dream that kills Richie. Through this character King examines the complexities inherent in all human relationships no matter how simple they appear. Even the most heroic act may have a dark side.

The Military

While King presents both positive and negative members of the mission to contain the threat of the aliens, a major source of evil in the novel is a member of this force. For the most part the men who are brought to Maine are ordinary people caught up in events they can only attempt to control. But the soldiers associated with Kurtz as members of his elite inner circle are as vicious as the weasels they destroy. They enjoy killing other human beings. Kurtz has picked these men and women, and they reflect his efficiency, his dedication, and his insanity. The basic conflict in the military operation comes from two longtime associates, Abraham Kurtz and Owen Underhill. They have served together before, and each knows the other quite well. Kurtz is the older and senior officer. While he appreciates Underhill's value to the team he is willing to destroy him because he has not exactly followed orders in the past. Kurtz represents the insanity of the military mind, and Underhill demonstrates the heroism and compassion that are its best points.

As Archie Perlmutter, another subordinate, suspects, Abraham Kurtz is too fortunate a coincidence to be the name of the commanding officer. He acknowledges the connections to characters from Joseph Conrad's "Heart of Darkness," and the film *Apocalypse Now*. While Perlmutter never discovers the truth, the reader learns that the man was born Robert Coonts. Kurtz has dealt with earlier visits of these aliens, and he seems to be the ideal choice for the person to lead the containment mission. He knows his soldiers and how to inspire them. Unfortunately he has bouts where his loss of control results in bizarre actions. He shoots the toe off a cook because the man used a racial epithet to characterize the aliens.

King states that Kurtz is not sane because he does not dream. He also fears the telepathic powers conferred by the aliens. Such powers represent his fear of a loss of control. He uses his ability to anticipate what others may do as a way to surprise and maintain his power over them. The aliens threaten this control, and he fights them fiercely. But he is even harder on his own men. He believes in never giving anyone a second chance, and he is angry because has done so for Underhill. When Underhill betrays him by leaving with Henry, the destruction of this man becomes his total focus. At the end he is destroyed because his own men know that they cannot trust him. Freddy kills Kurtz before his own commander turns on him.

Owen Underhill is another person whose life is defined by an incident from his childhood. Unlike the members of the group, he has done something that he regrets for the rest of his life. As a young boy of perhaps seven or eight he sees an ambulance arrive next door to take away the woman of the house, Mrs. Rapeloew, who has suffered a stroke. He notices that the family has left their front door open. At first he goes up to close it as a good Christian would, but he cannot resist the temptation to enter. Once in he is overcome by the urge to trash the place. He attempts to urinate on Mr. Rapeloew's toothbrush, pours water on the stove's electric burners, and smashes a serving platter before he leaves. He is haunted by these actions for the rest of his life. His decisions to help Henry, both in going after Mr. Gray and in letting the civilians have a chance to escape before they are slaughtered by Kurtz at Gosselin's store, are attempts at redemption. He manages to destroy the weasel before it gets into the water supply, and though Kurtz does kill him, Owen dies happy in the knowledge that he has become the hero he always wanted to be.

THEME

In his "Author's Note" at the end of *Dreamcatcher*, King acknowledges the "sublime release we find in vivid dreams" (619). The impact of dreams of all kinds is the thematic core of the novel. The dreamcatcher itself becomes a symbol of these dreams, but as a symbol it goes far beyond its source. The object has connections to the Native American heritage that is its origin, but it has also become an icon of popular culture available at crafts fairs and flea markets. Its use has mutated and adapted to the modern world just as those who fight the weasels fear these creatures will do in our world. Popular culture also has strong connections to the world of dreams. Once it is occupied by the military, Gosselin's store is lit so it looks like a movie set. Movies are prime examples of the ways that dreams and reality can be confused. And King himself has created a fictional world that takes on a kind of reality when it appears in novel after novel.

King constantly acknowledges his debt to other genre authors from Edgar Allan Poe to the present and the intensity of the fictional worlds they create. Horror as a genre constantly challenges the boundaries between what we know is real and what might possibly happen. Possibilities generate the fear that is part of the effect of this genre. Popular culture creates a world of shared experience that makes King's fictional world seem more real. When Ripley becomes the name of the alien growth in *Dreamcatcher*, readers familiar with the film *Alien* immediately understand the reference. It is a name that we appreciate because we share an awareness of its meaning in our lives. Even the weasels that emerge from bodies have common traits with the alien creatures that also come out of bodies in the *Alien* films. If we have seen these images on film they take on an additional reality, that of the photograph. While we know films can show worlds that do not exist, the fact that we see them gives them a life. King employs these elements to intensify the experience.

He also uses elements from his other novels in the same way. Derry has become a very real town to King's readers. When he refers to the way children have disappeared in Derry, he is referring to *It*. Mr. Gray uses Jonesy's memory of the Standpipe, the city's former water storage container and his first choice for a means of contaminating the water supply, but he does not know that it was destroyed at the end of *It*. These references to other works generate a sense of a fictional world whose breadth and depth are comparable to our own. Through his use of his own fiction, King extends the realm of the possible. We may even look on a map of Maine expecting to find the town that is so familiar to us.

But at the same time, in *Dreamcatcher* King also criticizes our belief in the reality of fictional worlds. Mr. Gray takes the form he does because Jonesy has expectations about aliens based on his experiences with films. Kurtz adopts his name because it expresses the personality he wants to present to the world based on associations with film and literature. He likes the combination of insanity and power that it represents. Popular culture can influence people in both positive and negative ways. It can help us understand and appreciate the world we live in, but it can also provide images that lead us to reproduce elements of that culture without thinking or analyzing experiences on our own. We can be drawn in the way that Jonesy is. He can only survive when he leaves the world that he has created. Or we can adopt images from other sources like Kurtz rather than expressing our own selves.

As King tells us in the novel, the dreamcatcher is also a kind of flytrap (495). Both the attraction and the danger in dreams lie in their seeming reality. Dreams can be a positive force. They help us survive hard times; they make us heroic. They give us the ability to see beyond the present. Those who don't dream, like Kurtz, cannot maintain their sanity. When the members of the group all join together to find Josie they experience life with an intensity whose absence will haunt them for the rest of their lives. But dreams can also destroy, as the group knows because of their experience with Richie. The very dreamcatcher that united them and enabled some of them to survive the aliens also joined them in dreaming

Richie's death. And even at the moment when they unite to find Josie, Henry questions the meaning of the experience. If this is all there is, then what is the meaning of existence?

Henry realizes that the dreamcatcher may have provided joy in his childhood, but it is also the source of the despair that finds expression in his desire to commit suicide. By the end of the novel he reaffirms the importance of the dreamcatcher. On some level the group does save the world. But on another, the threat was not as great as everyone originally thought. As Jonesy's experiences demonstrated, humans are too much for the aliens, a new power beyond their previous encounters in the universe. Henry understands that for either good or evil "we are a *species* living in the dreamcatcher" (616). Jonesy has a dreamcatcher hanging in his cabin as a kind of talisman to ward off evil. It is a symbol of the way that we can connect as human beings. If Henry wants to know if that is all there is, he doesn't realize that individual heroic moments may be the best we can hope for. If saving the world is an illusion, those times when we make a difference in the lives of those around us are important.

By the end of the novel King brings us to an understanding of the relevance of our everyday lives. Characters in popular culture may have opportunities to save the world. Through the dreamworlds of literature and film, we can get some sense of that kind of experience. But in our own lives we can connect with other people. And we can make those choices that place us with the group that stands up to the bullies of the world and save our own Duddits. We may not experience the telepathic communication of the members of the group joined by their connection to Duddits. But a novel like *Dreamcatcher* both allows us to briefly share that experience and then apply its importance in our own lives. At the end King brings us back to the everyday world of Jonesy and Henry. There is darkness awaiting us in the real world and the fictional world. One role of fiction is to show us ways to keep that darkness at bay.

ALTERNATIVE READING: TWO GENRES, HORROR AND SCIENCE FICTION

Genres are ways of both classifying and defining fictional experiences. A reader or viewer may select an experience based on previous contact and a set of expectations collected through that contact. Authors or film-makers employ certain genre conventions to best present their fiction. Publishers or producers label a work to satisfy the goals of the author and the expectations of the reader or viewer and to maximize their profits. Sometimes the choice is simple and at other times it is not as clear as it might be. The story is told that the producers of the first film in the *Alien* series were not certain whether to label the film horror or science fiction. The effect on the viewer was like that of the horror film, but it was set in the future. Science fiction films make more money because there is more repeat viewing of them. The phrase used on the first *Alien* posters seems to be an attempt to unite both genres: "In space no one can hear you scream." *Dreamcatcher* acknowledges its debt to *Alien*. And it certainly contains strong elements of the horror genre. The question then becomes, What kind of label should this book have?

One problem in the identification of either genre is the lack of a single definition that adequately covers works generally recognized to be a part of that genre. Science fiction is an especially broad category. The words "speculative" and "scientific" often appear. But some people do not even think that the genre has to deal with events occurring in the future. One of the problems with a definition that requires the use of the future is the way that time has of overtaking the fictional world. When we passed the year 1984, the novel of that name did not stop being science fiction. Most of those who attempt a definition seem to think that some connection between science and humanity is necessary and that the fiction should suggest a hypothetical world that may bear some connection to our world but is not really exactly like it. While some kind of science is necessary, the work need not focus on the world of science and may instead examine the sociological ramifications of changes in our societal structure.

There is no single clear definition of horror either. Many see the genre in terms of its effect on the audience. We expect to be frightened by contact with horror. Often the genre depends on the presence of some kind of monster, whether natural or supernatural. Modern horror can present a serial killer or a vampire as the source of terror. Horror is usually concerned with the nature of evil and the conflict between good and evil. Because of this conflict, some examples of the genre can use elements of religion. Generally we think of the world of this genre as dark with creatures hiding in the shadows.

King is best known as a novelist who writes horror fiction; most of his readers would categorize him this way. But there are instances when his fiction seems to cross genre boundaries. Some of his novels contain elements of science fiction even though they are generally seen as horror. *Tommyknockers* deals with an alien spaceship, but humans become monsters through contact with it. Recently such creations as the low men in yellow coats suggest a source of horror outside our known world. Certainly *Dreamcatcher* clearly presents creatures from another planet. King offers scientific information about these creatures and how they grow and spread. At one point Henry talks about different strains of the fungus, Ripley one and Ripley two, depending on the source of the contamination.

But unlike the film *Alien*, where the effect is that of a horror film even though it takes place in outer space, *Dreamcatcher* seems to transcend genre definitions rather than combining them. King's skill with both genres allows him to employ their structures to investigate those traits that make us human. He has begun this quest in such books as *Desperation*, in which he goes beyond the usual limits of horror to question the role of God. In *Dreamcatcher* he asks why we are good or evil outside the context of formal religion. He takes what he has learned about popular genres to explore our very humanity.

Bibliography

WORKS BY STEPHEN KING

Novels

Bag of Bones. New York: Scribner, 1998; New York: Pocket Books, 1999.

[With Peter Straub.] *Black House*. New York: Random House, 2001.

Carrie. Garden City, NY: Doubleday, 1974; New York: New American Library, 1975.

Christine. New York: Viking, 1983; New York: Signet, 1983.

Cujo. New York: Viking, 1981; New York: Signet, 1982.

Cycle of the Wolf. Westland, MI: Land of Enchantment, 1983; New York: New American Library, 1985.

The Dark Half. New York: Viking, 1989; New York: New American Library, 1990.

The Dark Tower: The Gunslinger. West Kingston, RI: Donald M. Grant, 1984; New York: New American Library, 1988.

The Dark Tower II: The Drawing of the Three. New York: New American Library, 1987.

The Dark Tower III: The Waste Lands. New York: New American Library, 1991.

The Dark Tower IV: Wizard and Glass. New York: Plume, 1997; New York: Signet, 1998.

The Dead Zone. New York: Viking, 1979; New York: New American Library, 1980.

Desperation. New York: Viking, 1996; New York: Signet, 1997.

Dolores Claiborne. New York: Viking, 1993; New York: New American Library, 1994.

Dreamcatcher. New York: Scribner, 2001.

The Eyes of the Dragon. New York: Viking, 1987; New York: New American Library, 1987.

Firestarter. New York: Viking, 1980; New York: New American Library, 1981.

Gerald's Game. New York: Viking, 1992; New York: New American Library, 1993.

The Girl Who Loved Tom Gordon. New York: Scribner, 1999; New York: Pocket Books, 2000.

The Green Mile. New York: Signet, 1997; New York: Pocket Books, 1999; New York: Scribner, 2000.

Hearts in Atlantis. New York: Scribner, 1999; New York: Pocket Books, 2000.

Insomnia. New York: Viking, 1994; New York: New American Library, 1995.

It. New York: Viking, 1986; New York: New American Library, 1987.

Misery. New York: Viking, 1987; New York: New American Library, 1987.

Needful Things. New York: Viking, 1991; New York: New American Library, 1992.

Pet Sematary. Garden City, NY: Doubleday, 1983; New York: New American Library, 1984.

Rose Madder. New York: Viking, 1995; New York: Signet, 1996.

'Salem's Lot. Garden City, NY: Doubleday, 1975; New York: New American Library, 1976.

The Shining. Garden City, NY: Doubleday, 1977; New York: New American Library, 1978.

The Stand. Garden City, NY: Doubleday, 1978; New York: New American Library, 1979; 2d ed., rev. and unexpurg., New York: Doubleday, 1990.

[With Peter Straub.] *The Talisman*. New York: Viking Press and G.P. Putnam's Sons, 1984; New York: Berkley, 1985.

The Tommyknockers. New York: G.P. Putnam's Sons, 1987; New York: New American Library, 1988.

Stephen King Writing As Richard Bachman

The Long Walk. New York: New American Library, 1979.

Rage. New York: New American Library, 1977.

The Regulators. New York: Dutton, 1996; New York: Signet, 1997.

Roadwork. New York: New American Library, 1981.

The Running Man. New York: New American Library, 1982.

Thinner. New York: New American Library, 1984.

Collections

The Bachman Books: Four Early Novels. New York: New American Library, 1985.

Creepshow. New York: New American Library, 1982.

Different Seasons. New York: Viking, 1982; New York: New American Library, 1983.

Four Past Midnight. New York: Viking, 1990; New York: New American Library, 1991.

Night Shift. Garden City, NY: Doubleday, 1978; New York: New American Library, 1983.

Nightmares and Dreamscapes. New York: Viking, 1993.

Skeleton Crew. New York: Putnam, 1985; New York: New American Library, 1986.

Nonfiction

Danse Macabre. New York: Everest House, 1981; New York: Berkley, 1982.

"Diamonds Are Forever." *Life* May 1994: 26–34.

"On Becoming a Brand Name," Foreword to *Fear Itself: The Early Works of Stephen King*. Ed. Tim Underwood and Chuck Miller. San Francisco: Underwood-Miller, 1993: 15–42.

On Writing: A Memoir of the Craft. New York: Scribner, 2000.

Rev. of *Hannibal*, by Thomas Harris. *New York Times Book Review* 13 June 1999: 4–6.

Rev. of *Harry Potter and the Goblet of Fire*, by J.K. Rowling. *New York Times Book Review* 23 July 2000: 13–14.

Secret Windows: Essays and Fiction of the Craft of Writing. New York: Book-of-the-Month Club, 2000.

"Son of the Best Seller Stalks the Moors." *New York Times Book Review* 6 June 1993, sec. 7: 59.

Screenplays

Cat's Eye

Creepshow

Golden Years

Maximum Overdrive

Pet Sematary

Silver Bullet

Sleepwalkers

The Stand

Storm of the Century. New York: Pocket Books, 1999.

WORKS ABOUT STEPHEN KING

General

Beahm, George, ed. *The Stephen King Companion*. Kansas City, MO: Andrews and McMeel, 1989.

———. *Stephen King Country*. Philadelphia, PA: Running Press, 1999.

Blue, Tyson. *The Unseen King*. Mercer Island, WA: Starmont House, 1989.

Browne, Ray, and Gary Hoppenstand, eds. *The Gothic World of Stephen King: Landscape of Nightmares*. Bowling Green, OH: Bowling Green State University Popular Press, 1987.

Burns, Gail E. "Women, Danger, and Death: The Perversion of the Female Principle in Stephen King's Fiction." In *Sexual Politics and Popular Culture*. Ed. Diane Raymond. Bowling Green, OH: Bowling Green State University Popular Press, 1990: 158–72.

Collings, Michael R. *The Films of Stephen King*. Mercer Island, WA: Starmont House, 1986.

———. *Infinite Explorations: Art and Artifice in Stephen King's* It, Misery, *and* The Tommyknockers. Mercer Island, WA: Starmont House, 1986.

———. *The Many Facets of Stephen King*. Mercer Island, WA: Starmont House, 1985.

———. *Stephen King as Richard Bachman*. Mercer Island, WA: Starmont House, 1985.

———. *The Stephen King Concordance*. Mercer Island, WA: Starmont House, 1985.

———. *The Stephen King Phenomenon*. Mercer Island, WA: Starmont House, 1986.

Collings, Michael R., and David A. Engebretson. *The Shorter Works of Stephen King*. Mercer Island, WA: Starmont House, 1985.

Connor, Jeff. *Stephen King Goes to Hollywood*. New York: New American Library, 1987.

Davis, Jonathan P. *Stephen King's America*. Bowling Green, OH: Bowling Green University Popular Press, 1994.

Docherty, Brian, ed. *American Horror Fiction: From Brockden Brown to Stephen King*. New York: St. Martin's, 1990.

Dubner, Stephen J. "The Demon in Stephen King." *New York Times Magazine* 13 Aug. 2000: 30–35.

Egan, James. "Apocalypticism in the Fiction of Stephen King." *Extrapolation* 25 (1984): 214–27.

———. "Sacral Parody in the Fiction of Stephen King." *Journal of Popular Culture* 23 (Winter 1989): 125–41.

———. " 'A Single Powerful Spectacle': Stephen King's Gothic Melodrama." *Extrapolation* 27 (1986): 62–75.

Gallagher, Bernard J. "Breaking Up Isn't Hard to Do: Stephen King, Christopher Lasch, and Psychic Fragmentation." *Journal of American Culture* 10 (Winter 1987): 59–67.

Herron, Don, ed. *Reign of Fear: Fiction and Film of Stephen King*. Los Angeles: Underwood-Miller, 1988.

Hohne, Karen A. "The Power of the Spoken Word in the Works of Stephen King." *Journal of Popular Culture* 28, no. 2 (1994): 93–103.

Horsting, Jessie. *Stephen King at the Movies*. New York: Starlog Press and New American Library, 1986.

Lloyd, Ann. *The Films of Stephen King*. New York: St. Martin's, 1994.

Magistrale, Tony, ed. *The Dark Descent: Essays Defining Stephen King's Horrorscape*. Westport, CT: Greenwood Press, 1992.

———. "Inherited Haunts: Stephen King's Terrible Children." *Extrapolation* 26 (1985): 43–49.

———. *Landscape of Fear: Stephen King's American Gothic*. Bowling Green, OH: Bowling Green State University Popular Press, 1988.

———. *The Moral Voyages of Stephen King*. Mercer Island, WA: Starmont House, 1989.

———. *Stephen King, the Second Decade*: Danse Macabre *to* The Dark Half. New York: Twayne, 1992.

Price, Robert M. "Fundamentalists in the Fiction of Stephen King." *Studies-in-Weird-Fiction* (Spring 1989): 12–14.

Reino, Joseph. *Stephen King, the First Decade: From* Carrie *to* Pet Sematary. Boston: Twayne, 1988.

Russell, Sharon A. *Stephen King: A Critical Companion*. Westport, CT: Greenwood Press, 1996.

Schweitzer, Darrell, ed. *Discovering Stephen King*. Mercer Island, WA: Starmont House, 1985.

Singer, Mark. "What Are You Afraid Of?" *New Yorker* 7 Sept. 1998: 56–67.

Spignesi, Stephen J. *The Complete Stephen King Encyclopedia*. Ann Arbor, MI: Popular Culture, Ink, 1993.

———. *The Lost Work of Stephen King: A Guide to Unpublished Manuscripts, Story Fragments, Alternative Versions, and Oddities*. Secaucus, NJ: Birch Lane Press, 1998.

Uncut. Sept. 2001: 13.

Underwood, Tim, and Chuck Miller, eds. *Fear Itself: The Early Works of Stephen King*. San Francisco: Underwood-Miller, 1993.

———. *Kingdom of Fear: The World of Stephen King*. New York: New American Library, 1986.

Winter, Douglas E. *The Reader's Guide to Stephen King*. Mercer Island, WA: Starmont House, 1982.

———. *Stephen King: The Art of Darkness*. New York: New American Library, 1986.

Biography

"Author as Star." *The Economist* 310 (18 Mar. 1989): 97.

Beahm, George. *The Stephen King Story*. Kansas City, MO: Andrews and McMeel, 1992.

Caldwell, Gail. "Stephen King: Bogeyman as Family Man." *Boston Globe*, 15 Apr. 1990: 1A+.

Davis, William A. "The Horror King of Bangor." *Boston Globe*, 31 Oct. 1990: 25.

Denison. D.C. "Stephen King." *Boston Globe*, 2 Aug. 1987: 2.

Geyelin, Milo, and Wade Lambert. "Stephen King." *Wall Street Journal*, 5 Oct. 1992: 3B.

Golden, Daniel, "Field of Screams." *Boston Globe*, 30 Aug. 1992: 14 BGM+.

"King Haunted by College Columns." *Boston Globe*, 5 Dec. 1990: 73.

Underwood, Tim, and Chuck Miller, eds. *Bare Bones: Conversations on Terror with Stephen King*. New York: Warner Books, 1989.

———. *Feast of Fear: Conversation with Stephen King*. New York: Warner Books, 1993.

Web Pages

Betts Bookstore: www.acadia.net/W95020.

Book-of-the-Month Club: www.stephenkinglibrary.com.

Books: www.3dham.com/bookstore/king.htm.

Books: www.best-authors-books.com/stephen_king.htm.

Fan site: www.matakoff.com/skc.htm.

Fan site: skingweb.virtualave.net.

Fan site: www.utopianweb.com/king.

Fan site: www.horrorking.com.

Official King Web site: www.stephenking.com.

Stephen King e-zine: spinejar.webjump.com.

Bag of Bones

Annichiarico, Mark. "*Bag of Bones*." *Library Journal* July 1998: 137.

Hand, Elizabeth. "*Bag of Bones*." *Fantasy & Science Fiction* May 1999: 41–46.

Jones, Malcolm, Jr. "A Scary Look at Love." *Newsweek* 21 Sept. 1998: 94–96.

Labi, Nadya. "*Bag of Bones*." *Time* 12 Oct. 1998: 116.

Lehmann-Haupt, Christopher. "Death, Terror and Writer's Block." *New York Times* 21 Sept. 1998: E6.

Olson, Ray. "*Bag of Bones*." *Booklist* 1 Sept. 1998: 6.

Rafferty, Terrence. "Stephen King's Big Chill." *GQ* Sept. 1998: 159+.

Webb, James Neal. "*Bag of Bones*." *BookPage Fiction Review*. Online. ProMotion. 23 April 1999. www.bookpage.com.

The Dark Tower IV: Wizard and Glass

Olson, Ray. "*Wizard and Glass*." *Booklist* 93, Aug. 1997: 1847.

"*Wizard and Glass*." *Kirkus Reviews* 65, 1 Aug. 1997: 1138.

Desperation and *The Regulators*

Angell, Robert. "The Tak of the Town." *New Yorker* 30 Sept. 1996: 78+.

Annichiarico, Mark. "*The Regulators/Desperation*." *Library Journal* July 1996: 152.

Mohonk Hotel: www.mohonk.com.

Olson, Ray. "*The Regulators* by Richard Bachman." *Booklist* July 1996: 1779.

———. "*Desperation* by Stephen King." *Booklist* Aug. 1996: 1854.

Roush, Matt. "King's Double House of Horrors." *USA Today* 24 Sept. 1996: D1.

Steinberg, Sybil S. "*Desperation.*" *Publishers Weekly* 24 July 1996: 43.

Dreamcatcher

Geary, Robert F. "Terrors Alien and Domestic." *The World & I* July 2001: 224–229.

Harrison, Colin. "Weasel from Another Planet." *New York Times Book Review* 15 Apr. 2001: 6.

Maslin, Janet. "A Fateful Step Off a Curb and into Alien Territory." *New York Times* 15 Mar. 2001: B9.

The Girl Who Loved Tom Gordon

Burns, Ann. "*The Girl Who Loved Tom Gordon.*" *Library Journal* 15 Feb. 2000: 139.

De Lint, Charles. "*The Girl Who Loved Tom Gordon.*" *Fantasy & Science Fiction* Sept. 1999: 28–29.

Lehmann-Haupt, Christopher. "A Modern Fairy Tale of the Dark North Woods." *New York Times* 15 Apr. 1999: E9.

Smothers, Bonnie. "*The Girl Who Loved Tom Gordon.*" *Booklist* 1 Apr. 1999: 1366.

The Green Mile

Delingpole, James. "A King One Hates to Love." *Spectator* 21 Nov. 1998: 50.

Handy, Bruce. "Monster Writer." *Time* 2 Sept. 1996: 60.

Lehmann-Haupt, Christopher. "Why 'To Be Continued' Is Continued." *New York Times* 7 Apr. 1996: 2+.

Polito, Robert. "Apocalypse Now." *New York Times Book Review* 20 Oct. 1996: 16.

Sutherland, John. "Off To Old Sparky." *TLS* 27 Nov. 1998: 22.

Hearts in Atlantis

Crain, Caleb. "There but for Fortune." *New York Times Book Review* 12 Sept. 1999: 10.

De Lint, Charles. "*Hearts in Atlantis.*" *Fantasy & Science Fiction* Mar. 2000: 26–27.

Hand, Elizabeth. "America's Gothic Master Spreads His Wings." *Village Voice* 30 Nov. 1999: 88–90.

Kaveney, Roz. "*Hearts in Atlantis.*" *New Statesman* 6 Dec. 1999: 78+.

OTHER BOOKS ON HORROR

Clover, Carol J. *Men, Women, and Chainsaws: Gender in the Modern Horror Film.* Princeton, NJ: Princeton University Press, 1992.

Gelder, Ken, ed. *The Horror Reader.* London: Routledge, 2000.

Heller, Terry. *The Delights of Terror: An Aesthetics of the Tale of Terror.* Urbana: University of Illinois Press, 1987.

Holman, C. Hugh, and William Harmon. "Regionalism." *A Handbook to Literature.* New York: Macmillan, 1992: 399.

Jackson, Rosemary. *Fantasy: The Literature of Subversion.* London: Methuen, 1981.

Todorov, Tzvetan. *The Fantastic: A Structural Approach to a Literary Genre.* Trans. Richard Howard. Ithaca, NY: Cornell University Press, 1973.

Waller, Gregory A. *American Horrors: Essays on the Modern American Horror Film.* Urbana: University of Illinois Press, 1987.

Index

About the Author

SHARON A. RUSSELL is Professor of Communication and Women's Studies at Indiana State University, where she teaches courses on film and television. She has published extensively on horror film and literature and detective fiction. She is the author of *Stephen King: A Critical Companion* (Greenwood Press, 1996). She has also written *The Guide to African Cinema*.

Critical Companions to Popular Contemporary Writers
First Series—*also available on CD-ROM*

V.C. Andrews *by E.D. Huntley*

Tom Clancy *by Helen S. Garson*

Mary Higgins Clark *by Linda C. Pelzer*

Arthur C. Clarke *by Robin Anne Reid*

James Clavell *by Gina Macdonald*

Pat Conroy *by Landon C. Burns*

Robin Cook *by Lorena Laura Stookey*

Michael Crichton *by Elizabeth A. Trembley*

Howard Fast *by Andrew Macdonald*

Ken Follett *by Richard C. Turner*

John Grisham *by Mary Beth Pringle*

James Herriot *by Michael J. Rossi*

Tony Hillerman *by John M. Reilly*

John Jakes *by Mary Ellen Jones*

Stephen King *by Sharon A. Russell*

Dean Koontz *by Joan G. Kotker*

Robert Ludlum *by Gina Macdonald*

Anne McCaffrey *by Robin Roberts*

Colleen McCullough *by Mary Jean DeMarr*

James A. Michener *by Marilyn S. Severson*

Anne Rice *by Jennifer Smith*

Tom Robbins *by Catherine E. Hoyser and Lorena Laura Stookey*

John Saul *by Paul Bail*

Erich Segal *by Linda C. Pelzer*

Gore Vidal *by Susan Baker and Curtis S. Gibson*

813   Russell, Sharon A.,
R   1941-

           Revisiting Stephen
           King.

$34.95   11/20/2002

DATE			

BAKER & TAYLOR